Praise for
Alejandro Jodorowsky
and His Works

"No one alive today, anywhere, has been able to demonstrate the sheer possibilities of artistic invention—and in so many disciplines—as powerfully as Alejandro Jodorowsky."

NPR Books

"Alejandro Jodorowsky is a demiurge and an interpreter of our stories, always exploring further the understanding of both the beauty and complexity revealed by humankind."

Diana Widmaier Picasso, art historian

"Jodorowsky is a brilliant, wise, gentle, and cunning wizard with tremendous depth of imagination and crystalline insight into the human condition."

Daniel Pinchbeck, author of
Breaking Open the Head

"Alejandro Jodorowsky seamlessly and effortlessly weaves together the worlds of art, the confined social structure, and things we can only touch with an open heart and mind."

Erykah Badu, artist and alchemist

"One of the most inspiring artists of our time. . . . A prophet of creativity."

KANYE WEST, RECORDING ARTIST

"*The Dance of Reality* begs to be read as a culminating work. . . ."

LOS ANGELES TIMES

"*The Dance of Reality* [film] is a trippy but big-hearted reimagining of the young Alejandro's unhappy childhood in a Chilean town. . . ."

NEW YORK TIMES MAGAZINE

"*Manual of Psychomagic* is great . . . like a cookbook of very useful recipes that can help us to understand our life and the universe we live in."

MARINA ABRAMOVIĆ, PERFORMANCE ARTIST

"His films *El Topo* and *The Holy Mountain* were trippy, perverse, and blasphemous."

WALL STREET JOURNAL

"The best movie director ever!"

MARILYN MANSON, MUSICIAN, ACTOR, AND MULTIMEDIA ARTIST

THE
FINGER
AND THE
MOON

Zen Teachings and Koans

Alejandro Jodorowsky

Translated by Alberto Tiburcio Urquiola

Inner Traditions
Rochester, Vermont • Toronto, Canada

Inner Traditions
One Park Street
Rochester, Vermont 05767
www.InnerTraditions.com

Certified Sourcing
www.sfiprogram.org
SFI-00854

Text stock is SFI certified

Originally published in French under the title *Le doigt et la lune* by
    Éditions Albin Michel
First U.S. edition published in 2016 by Inner Traditions

Library of Congress Cataloging-in-Publication Data

Names: Jodorowsky, Alejandro, author.
Title: The finger and the moon : Zen teachings and koans / Alejandro
    Jodorowsky ; translated by Alberto Tiburcio Urquiola.
Other titles: Doight et la lune. English
Description: Rochester, Vermont : Inner Traditions, 2016. | Includes
index.
Identifiers: LCCN 2016016201 (print) | LCCN 2016036006 (e-book) |
ISBN 9781620555354 (pbk.) | ISBN 9781620555361 (e-book)
Subjects: LCSH: Zen Buddhism. | Zen stories. | Haiku. | Koan. |
Takata, Ejo, –1997.
Classification: LCC BQ9265.4 .J6313 2016 (print) |
LCC BQ9265.4 (e-book) | DDC 294.3/420427—dc23
LC record available at https://lccn.loc.gov/2016016201

Printed and bound in the United States by Lake Book Manufacturing, Inc.
The text stock is SFI certified. The Sustainable Forestry Initiative®
program promotes sustainable forest management.

10 9 8 7 6 5 4 3 2 1

Text design and layout by Priscilla Baker
This book was typeset in Garamond Premier Pro with Chaparral,
Novarese, and Legacy Sans used as display typefaces

CONTENTS

ZEN AND JAPANESE STORIES

———— ————

KOANS

HAIKUS

PROLOGUE

During the late 1950s, Zen master Yamada Mumon sent his disciple Ejo Takata from Japan to visit a North American *zendo* in, if I remember correctly, San Francisco. Once there, following his master's orders, he looked for a location to found a Zen Rinzai school. His method of searching—since he spoke only Japanese—consisted of *not* looking for it. He stood at the edge of a road and decided to establish the school wherever he was dropped off by the first vehicle to give him a ride. A truck carrying oranges left him in Mexico City with no clothes other than his *koromo* (monastic robe) and just ten dollars in his pocket. In that immense city of twenty million people, he wandered through the streets for an hour until a psychoanalyst, a disciple of psychologist Erich Fromm, happened to drive down the road. Fromm is the author of, among other things, a book called *Zen Buddhism and Psychoanalysis,* and at that time he had just discovered Zen through the works of D. T. Suzuki.

The psychoanalyst was surprised—or, more precisely, astonished—to see a Japanese man calmly wandering the streets of Mexico City and invited Takata to join him in the car. He considered the monk's arrival to be a major event in the development of his new school. Along with a group of physicians and psychoanalysts, he installed Takata, who would eventually become my master, in a zendo on the outskirts of the capital.

At that time all that we knew about Zen had come from some books that had been poorly translated into Spanish. The *koans* appeared to our logical spirits as unresolvable mysteries. And we imagined an "enlightened" Zen master to be a wizard capable of answering all our metaphysical doubts, and even of giving us the power to defeat death.

After struggling quite a bit to get in touch with the master, one fine day, shaking with excitement, I finally knocked at his door. A smiling Asian man with a shaved head, of uncertain age—he could have been in his twenties or his sixties—and wearing monk's attire, opened the door and immediately treated me as though I had been his lifelong friend. He took me by the hand, led me to the meditation room, and showed me a piece of white cloth hanging on the wall inscribed with a Japanese word he hastily translated and pronounced with difficulty: happiness.

This is how my experience with Ejo Takata started. That year I wrote down some impressions that—however naïve and despite being expressed by an idealistic teenager—have never ceased, in my view, to be valid. Years have passed, but the respectful love I professed to Ejo Takata has never disappeared from what I can simply call "my soul." My interpretations of the stories and koans originate from my encounter with this both great and humble master. (About his life in Japan, I know nothing but this anecdote: While the Americans were bombing Tokyo, in the middle of a rain of bombs, he continued meditating.)

Experience with Ejo Takata
(Mexico, 1961)

The first time I went to the zendo, the master showed me a poem that ended like this:

> *He who has nothing but feet will contribute*
> *with his feet.*
> *He who has nothing but eyes will contribute*
> *with his eyes to this great spiritual work.*
> *Throughout his prayers, the master coughs*
> *and sneezes. I just try to meditate,*
> *barely daring to breathe.*
> *The master no longer prays.*
> *These chants are him. The prayers cough*
> *and sneeze.*

The student meditated in a corner of the zendo. Fearing that it might become a habit, he went to the opposite corner.

He passed through the four corners of the zendo, and through all the places where people meditated. The master always meditated in the same place; however, nothing was done by rote.

The disciple insisted on taking off his shoes before entering the zendo, with its hardwood floor. He had dirtied his feet. As he sat down on the wooden parquet, he stained it.

The master only took off his shoes when he sat in his place.

When he went to the master's house, the disciple took off his shoes so that he would not stain the floor, but when he visited his friends, he didn't even bother to wipe the soles of his shoes on the mat at the entrance.

The master invited the disciple to sit in the garden. He took out a straw chair and brought it. But halfway through, he gave the chair to the disciple.

The master said,

> *"From Mexico City we can see*
> *Popocatepetl.* But from Popocatepetl*
> *we can't admire Popocatepetl."*

When the master prayed, his words produced a musical vibration. I was grateful for this sound because it made my cells vibrate; it put them in order, like a magnet, in one direction. The words became irrelevant to me.

Before departing, the master wanted to give me his cane—the *keisaku*—as a gift.

These were my feelings: "If you have a cane, I'll take it from you; if you don't, I'll give one to you. Oh, infinite mercy! I do not thank you. I didn't have one and you wanted to give it to me. Now I have it, so take it away from me. Only thus would you have truly given it to me. Allow me to refuse your gift. One day my hands will blossom, and I will not need a cane because I will be able to strike your shoulder with my palm (and with my fingers)."

---

*A volcano near Mexico City

The master said: "If you do a good deed and you tell some-one about it, you lose any benefit it might have brought to you." But he boasted about every good deed he did. He advertised it, not out of vanity but to avoid any inner gain for himself.

He wanted to do good without asking for anything in return.

A temple is not the "exclusive" place of the sacred. We go to the temple to learn the sense of the sacred. If the lesson has been understood, the entire earth becomes a temple, every man becomes a priest, and every food is a Communion host.

The master strikes me twice on the shoulder with his keisaku, which is a long, thin cane with a flat end. It has Japanese characters engraved on both ends. I ask him what they mean.

The characters on the striking end say, "I can't teach you anything. Learn by yourself—you know!" The characters on the other end say, "Grass blossoms in spring."

The master adds, "First, meditation, then comes spring and everything blossoms."

Suddenly, the master touches the disciple's mouth and asks him, "Why is it injured?" The disciple replies, "I had an accident."

And the master says, "One day your eyes will be very beautiful."

The Essential Sound of Emptiness

*The disciple approaches the master and asks,
"What is the essential sound of emptiness?"*

*The master replies, "What is the essential
sound of emptiness?"*

*"You are the master. I don't know the
answer, that's why I'm asking."*

*The master strikes him on the head. The
disciple becomes enlightened.*

The master has ceased to be identified with his ego; he has surrendered himself to emptiness, to inner silence. The only sound that resonates within him is his disciple's question. The latter mistakes the master's answer with the question he asks his own intellect, without realizing that the master does nothing but imitate him.

"You are the master. I don't know the answer; that's why I'm asking."

This is an absurd answer. The master doesn't want to ask him a question but imitates the sound of his words, devoid of any meaning. The disciple seeks concepts; he doesn't want to quit his intellectual pursuit. The master, striking his head, interrupts the flow of words. In just an instant the spirit becomes wordless.

Finally the disciple understands.

The master is no longer a person.

Everything else, the world, is the essential sound of emptiness. When the self ceases to exist, the world exists.

ZEN AND JAPANESE STORIES

Swallowing the Serpent

One day in a Zen monastery, a great master showed up unexpectedly. The cook had to immediately prepare him food. He hastily picked some vegetables from the garden in order to chop them up and make a tasty soup. The guest ate the soup. He savored it until the point when he found a serpent's head in his spoon. He summoned the cook for an explanation. The latter, upon seeing the serpent, extended his arm toward it, picked it up, and, to everyone's astonishment, swallowed it at once. He then turned around and in a dignified manner returned to the kitchen without uttering a word.

By swallowing the serpent right away, the cook was, in fact, swallowing his mistake. In general, we aren't ready to do the same.

On one occasion, as I was doing a tarot reading for Ejo Takata, I told him, "Listen, Ejo, I'm sorry to tell you this, you're a monk, you're a master, but according to this tarot you have sexual problems."

He wasn't defensive about it; he didn't distort things, nor did he seek to justify himself. He swallowed the serpent's head. He lifted his fist, crying out, "I do!" The next day he left for Japan to look for his wife.

The Two Cat Doors

A Japanese artist had two cats, a big one and a small one. He put two cat entrances in his door, one large and one small. A friend who was passing by was surprised.

"Why two cat entrances, when one would've been enough?"

"How so? There's one for each cat."

"Come on! A big one would've worked well for the two of them."

"True. I didn't think of it."

This is a rather weird story. I found it in a little book, *The Cat and the Samurai: Stories from Japan.** It's a collection of initiation-rite stories that defy logic.

In this next one there are two kinds of language: that of the heart and that of the intellect.

The artist had two cats, whereas the intellectual had none. How could the latter have guessed the love that the artist felt for his cats?

We could think that the artist's response reveals a simplistic way of thinking, or we could think that it means, "I don't use the intellect in the realm of love. The intellect has no place in the language of the heart. I want to honor my two cats by providing an entrance for each. If the small one bypasses

---

*Le chat et la samourai, contes du Japon, by Perusat Stork (Éditions Publisud, 1989).

the large entryway, that's his problem. He does as he wishes. Perhaps one day the bigger one will foolishly try to squeeze himself through the smaller entryway. What I care about is providing an entrance for each of them."

We each have a door that corresponds to us. We can't all go through the same one, however large it may be.

This reminds me that in popular imagery, Saint Peter's keychain has many keys. We may wonder why he has so many. Does paradise have that many doors? I have found an answer. Saint Peter has so many keys because we each come with our own. Saint Peter keeps the keys of those who have already gone into heaven. Supposing for a moment that paradise does exist, this means that you have your own entrance and can't use anyone else's.

Kafka wrote a short story about this. A man sought entry to the halls of justice, but the guard wouldn't allow him inside. He waited by the door for years, even bribing the guard, but the guard rejected him every time. When he was finally old and dying, the man asked why, even though everyone seeks justice, he had never seen anyone else come to the door. The guard answered that it had been created exclusively for him, and would now be shut.

Saint Peter's keychain is a positive version of Kafka's story, but the idea is the same. In the former, you have the key and you enter; in Kafka's version, you don't have the key.

The Fool and the Theologian

A Zen monk lived with his one-eyed brother, who was a fool. On a day that a famous theologian was coming from afar to speak with the monk, he was forced to be absent. He said to his brother, "Welcome and treat this wise man well. But above all, don't say a word to him and everything will be alright."

The monk then left the monastery. When he returned, he immediately went to see his guest.

"Has my brother welcomed you?" he asked.

Enthusiastically, the theologian replied, "Your brother is a fine person. He is a great theologian."

Surprised, the monk mumbled back, "What? My brother . . . a theologian?"

"We had a passionate discussion," the wise man went on, "expressing ourselves only through gestures. I showed him a finger, he replied showing me two. I then responded, as expected, by showing him three, and he left me baffled by showing me a clenched fist and ending the debate. With one finger I indicated the unity of Buddha. With two he widened my point of view, reminding me that Buddha could not be separated from his doctrine. Pleased with the reply, I showed him three fingers, signifying Buddha and his doctrine in the world. And then he gave me this sublime reply, showing me his fist: Buddha, his doctrine in the world, is part of a whole. It was thrilling."

Soon after, the monk went to see his one-eyed brother and demanded, "Tell me what happened with the theologian!"

"Quite simple," said the brother. "He provoked me,

showing me one finger to point out that I had only one eye. Not wanting to give in to his provocation, I replied that he was lucky to have two. He went on sarcastically to say that adding up all our eyes, we have three eyes. That was the last straw. Showing him a clenched fist, I threatened to make him into a corpse if he didn't stop his ill-intentioned innuendos. "

This story reflects the kinds of conversations we have between us. We think we're speaking about the same thing when in reality we're speaking about the opposite. We argue passionately, thinking we are communicating intimately with one another, but in the end we don't talk about anything. Each of us uses a language for the deaf. We all speak only about ourselves.

The other day someone referred to Simone de Beauvoir in my presence: Simone de Beauvoir this, Simone de Beauvoir that . . . "Which Simone de Beauvoir do you mean?" I asked. It's not enough to quote someone; it's important to specify what aspect of that person you're referencing. Every time we talk about someone, we speak of that person as if our perception is the same for everyone.

When someone speaks to me about the tarot, I try to figure out which tarot. There are so many! Likewise, I try to define what kind of interpretation the person has in mind.

Define for me who Simone de Beauvoir is to you, and then I'll give you my definition. We need to agree on the terms before going further. Without clarifying this beforehand, all our conversations are similar to that of the one-eyed fool with the theologian.

Crossing the River

A Zen master used to say, "When some people have to cross the river on a raft, they begin their passage, but soon after, they lose sight of their goals. They stay on the raft; it has become their goal."

People learn to read the tarot thinking that the goal is to learn to read it. The tarot is the raft. The goal is happiness.

Some think the goal is making money, but the goal is happiness. We have to make money with something we truly love, with something we love with passion. We might say we should do things that give us such intense pleasure that we would even do them for free. We have to ask for compensation for this work that we would do free of charge. We should make a living doing what we like to do.

Money is divine energy. That said, in our society it is considered the worst thing there is. And yet we're bound to use it to function in the world, to earn it and spend it. Why feel guilty when you earn a lot? What is the point of playing down the amount of our earnings? It's not difficult for me to imagine Christ blessing the world with a $500 bill in his hand. If you can't imagine this, ask yourself what sort of ideas you have on this issue.

I've seen blame heaped on money in both Catholic and Marxist families. According to them, we have the right to earn money up to a certain point. Once we pass that point, we become exploiters. We have to be poor and limited. Having more is forbidden.

I recently came across someone claiming to hate money, who has nonetheless lived off the money of others. No matter how much we may abhor money, we need it to live.

This energy can be used in a positive or negative way, to construct or deconstruct things.

Eyes Wide Open

A disciple asked his master, "Master, how do I reach the state of enlightenment?"

"It's very simple," replied the master. "To reach it, you need to do exactly what you do every day to make the sun rise."

Baffled, the disciple scratched his neck, wondering what he could do to make the sun rise. After thinking about it for a while, he arrived at the conclusion that he didn't really do anything, strictly speaking.

"But then why study calligraphy, karate, kendo, or archery? What's the point of ikebana *(flower arranging), preparing the bonsai, and so on?" he asked the master. "What is all that worth?"*

"So that when the sun rises, you will really have your eyes wide open."

We need to pay a lot of attention to what we really are, to be conscious about the sun we carry within us. To achieve it, we need to work diligently and deeply and practice many exercises to develop awareness and focus. Being awake means being awake to our own sun.

This is why we work so much—to allow things to reveal themselves by themselves.

What do we do to develop self-awareness? To me, there are two paths we must take simultaneously.

The first path consists of developing awareness of our own selves—working on ourselves until we reach the state of emptiness. When we achieve that, the universe will reveal itself inside us. Through this practice we widen our scope and deepen, intensify, and work on our own ideas, feelings, thoughts, desires, and material life. We work to achieve emptiness.

Simultaneously, in our relationship with the exterior, we work on unity in order to reach our own plenitude. That is to say, we work to dissolve ourselves into the totality. That is the second path.

Meditation consists, therefore, on being the whole and the void—on being everything, on being nothing. If we work so much it is partly to unite ourselves with the totality, the totality of the being, of the manifestation and the non-manifestation. And on the other hand, we do it to reach our own essential emptiness, which is the same totality.

There is my enlightenment. It is simple and complex at the same time.

The Monks and the Rabbits

Two monks were sitting outside in nature. One was surrounded by rabbits and the other wasn't. The monk not surrounded by rabbits said to the other one, "You are a saint. It's incredible! All of the rabbits are surrounding you, while they flee from me. What is your secret?"

"I have no secret. I just don't eat rabbits. That's all."

If you want another being to trust you, speak to it as if you were the clearest mirror. In the Gallery of Mineralogy and Geology of the Jardin des Plantes in Paris, there is the most beautiful obsidian mirror in all of Europe. You should come to resemble that mirror and reflect others without criticism or projection.

Miracle and Faith

Two disciples were talking. The first one said, with an attitude of superiority, "My master can cross the river walking on the water. Can yours perform miracles as mine does?"

The other humbly responded, "The biggest miracle my master does is not to do them."

Back in the days when I had no faith, I prayed, "God, please make a rose appear in my hand. I swear that if this happens I won't tell anyone, it will remain between you and me, but please, respond."

It was such a stupid attitude. Faith consists precisely of believing without proof. If you look for signs, for miraculous happenings, it shows you have no faith.

I would be no better if, like Sai Baba, I started manifesting holy ash in my hands. Only those who are dissatisfied with themselves and wish to prove to themselves that there is something greater than they are feel attracted to these kinds of miracles.

I am satisfied with who I am. I will have to live what I have to live. Only God will decide on the span of my existence, whatever this may be. Whether God enlightens me or not, I accept it. If a rose appears on my hand and I levitate, that's God's will. If nothing like this occurs, nothing happens. This changes nothing for me.

The Zen Garden

A Zen master asked his disciple to clean up the garden of the monastery. The disciple cleaned the garden and left it in an impeccable state, but the master wasn't satisfied. He had the disciple clean it a second time, and then a third time. Discouraged, the disciple complained, "But Master, there is nothing left to put in order or to clean up in this garden. Everything is done."

"There's one thing missing," replied the master. He shook a tree and some leaves came off, covering the ground.

"Now the garden is perfect," he concluded.

There is an orderly aspect of the mental dimension that allows the intellect to work within the order, and a disorderly aspect that allows the unconscious to manifest itself. Perfect order exists only alongside disorder. Absolute order in a garden kills the garden.

Attention

During a performance of Noh theater, a great actor was performing when suddenly, among the silent spectators, a well-known general shouted out right in the middle of the show. Everyone was displeased by this inappropriate interruption. Once the show had ended, people asked the actor what he had felt in that moment, and he responded, "The general was right. His shout put me back in character when I was losing concentration. To be precise, I was staring at a lamp that was about to fall. I became distracted and he noticed it."

The general was a warrior who immediately perceived a shortcoming in the actor. For a true warrior, a shortcoming like this can mean passing from life to death.

An evolved being has developed his capacity to pay attention. Those who haven't developed this skill cannot focus on something steadily. They are in a place without really being in it.

Paying attention is paying attention to others and to oneself. It is with this attitude that we meditate. Meditation and contemplation consist only of fixing our attention on what we really are. We start by fixing our attention on what we are, and we persevere until we find ourselves.

Ignorance and Enlightenment

Toward the end of Master Joshu's life, a disciple asked him, "If we speak about ignorance or enlightenment, it's like a children's game, making too much noise for nothing. Isn't it so, Master? Tell us what the real word is."

Joshu, that great old man, replied, "Perhaps the real word is not to say either of these two words: ignorance and enlightenment."

"Master," his disciple insisted, "leave these two words behind. Tell us the real word."

And Joshu replied, "Om burin pach!"

Which means nothing. It is nothing but a succession of meaningless sounds. Thus it is the real word. In other words, truth is unutterable. It is not a concept.

When we find ourselves, we find ourselves in what we are, without definition. This cannot be conceptualized.

The Interview

Governor Ichi went to visit Master Chuei-ien. Once at the monastery, he gave his title and requested an interview with the master. Chuei-ien absolutely refused to receive this illustrious character and had someone tell his visitor that Governor Ichi didn't exist. Having understood the message, the visitor again requested an interview, this time announcing himself only by his name. The wise man received him immediately.

Titles and positions are of secondary importance. What matters is what we really are, here and now. We have to see that immediately.

Hell and Paradise

A samurai asked a master to explain the difference between heaven and hell. Without responding, the master began insulting him. The samurai furiously drew his sword to behead the master.

"There you have hell," said the master before the samurai could execute the action. Impressed by these words, the warrior instantly calmed down and sheathed his sword.

As he did this, the master added, "There you have heaven."

We create our own hell when we enter certain states of mind, and conversely, we create our own paradise entering other states of mind. Hell and paradise depend on us.

Pay Attention

"Master, what do I need to do to learn the art of the sword?"
"You have to pay attention."
"Just that?"
"No, you have to pay more attention and more attention."
"Is that all I need?"
"No, you need more attention, more attention, and more attention."

It's all about constant attention. Like the crouching tiger with unwavering awareness, you look ahead, you observe yourself. You observe your values. You observe your truth with the insatiable desire to nourish yourself from within your being. You don't do this selfishly. You want to nourish yourself from your own true self, because within it lies the true self of the universe.

In this observation of every instant, discovering the smallest flaw makes you happy. You cry with emotion thinking you can fix it. You can overcome it. It's a job that your essential self encourages you to do.

You discover flaws, but you can also discover values.

An Impassive Old Man

A powerful warrior led his army on an invasion of a neighboring country. Since he was preceded by his reputation, nobody dared challenge him. Everyone fled his approach. One day, in a small town, he entered a temple and found inside a man of uncertain age sitting, unmoved, in lotus position. The warrior, interpreting the motionless presence of the old man as a challenge, drew his sword.

"Do you know who you are facing, you shameless grandfather? I could pierce your heart with this sword in the blink of an eye."

Without the slightest sign of worry, the old man replied, "And you, who are you facing? I could let you pierce my heart in the blink of an eye."

I have imagined the warrior plunging his sword into the old man's heart and the old man dying without blinking. How beautiful! This reminds me of a real Sufi story.

A Sufi was giving a talk about God. While he was explaining that everything is God, a man ambushed and murdered him. As he lay dying, the saint stared at his murderer and said to him with compassion, "You, too, are God."

It is the gift of oneself, the releasing of the ego. I wouldn't be capable of it. I would jump like a flea. I would defend myself with all my strength. I am not in a saintly state.

I have also imagined the warrior. After killing the old

man, he cut off his hair bun, just as samurais do when they find someone stronger than themselves. And from then on, his life was transformed. By inserting his sword into such a center of love, such a gift of self, the warrior experienced a great transformation.

A legend says that roses came out of the spear that was used to pierce Christ's side during the crucifixion. Also, according to the legend, the guard who wielded the spear suffered from cataracts, which were healed after his action. At this, the man changed and became enlightened. By inserting his violence, his murderous desire, into a center of love, he achieved self-realization.

Self-realization can be achieved by passing through violence, as long as the person on the receiving end of violence is a self-realized person.

The Test of the Jar

A sword master presented his three sons to a reputed master of weaponry in order to show him their level of development in this art. He placed a clay jar above a half-open door and summoned the youngest of his sons. When the youngest son opened the door, he caused the jar to tilt and fall. But before the jar could break against the floor, the lad had already taken his sword and beheaded the object. The father, turning toward the master, acknowledged that this son was not yet perfect.

He placed another jar over the half-open door and summoned his second son. This one drew his sword in the blink of an eye and broke the jar long before it reached the ground.

"My second son has reached a superior level," the father noted.

He repeated the drill with his oldest son. Instead of drawing his sword, the eldest son took the falling jar and placed it delicately on the ground. The father said, "This one has reached the highest level."

The master of weaponry, having witnessed the feats of the three sons, placed the jar over the door and summoned his best student. Peeking in through the opening of the door, the student smiled in amusement and, showing that he understood his master's intention, did not open the door.

With the oldest son we can see that when we master something, we no longer destroy anything. But once we reach the level of the fourth one, the master's student, we reach perfection. Then we don't even fall into the trap. We no longer need to solve the problem because we avoid it. He who achieves perfection in the art of the sword never needs to use his weapon. He dissolves the fight even before it starts. He can see it coming from a mile away.

The Head of the Dog

A samurai was walking with his dog one day when suddenly, baring his teeth for the first time, the dog started to bark furiously in his direction. Surprised and annoyed, the samurai drew his sword and cut off the animal's head. However, instead of falling to the ground, the head flew toward a tree behind the warrior and seized within its jaws a serpent that wanted to bite the samurai. Understanding thus that his dog had been warning him against an imminent threat, the helpless samurai lamented his irreparable gesture.

The dog wasn't attacking his master; he was warning him about danger. The samurai misinterpreted the animal's intentions. We have to know how to interpret things. Oftentimes people misinterpret an anecdote, and then, taking their version as fact, they rework it to make it into reality.

In any case, we can take reality for a dream. One day a woman was talking to me about the death of her father-in-law. I told her, "If you have never been able to express your hatred of your father-in-law, do it now. Go over to the wall and pray. Express your hatred first and then express your love."

"I have no account to settle with my father-in-law," the woman said. "My beef is with my husband. He announced the death in a brutal way."

"So you have a beef with your husband. Take this problem as a dream and interpret it. Take reality as a dream. Interpret it. This will help you understand what you feel."

The Learning Process

*"Master, I want to learn the art of the sword. How many years
will I need?"*

"Ten years."

"But that's too many!"

"Well then, twenty."

"But that's outrageous!"

"Thirty."

Without patience, you can't achieve anything. You've got to
keep going calmly, and eventually things will come.

In the end, time doesn't matter. You've got to understand
that an evolved creature lives not *in* time, but *with* time. He
is time. What difference does it make to him to do something twenty-six years from now or immediately, as long as he
does it?

KOANS

Regarding Koan Masters and Disciples

Koans usually involve a master and disciple together. I can imagine the master completely calm and relaxed and the disciple tense and nervous. A guru who is nervous and controls himself is not a real master; he's a disciple. On the other hand, if he scratches his bottom, he's a master. Joshu has expressed this idea in a wonderful phrase: "When the normal, ordinary man learns, he becomes a wise man; and when a wise man learns, he becomes a normal, ordinary man."

A historical anecdote about Joshu tells the way in which this master experienced his teachings in everyday life.

> *Someone came to visit Joshu for the first time. The visitor saw a magnificent old man meditating at the end of the garden. He asked the gardener, who was nearby, whether that old man was Joshu. And the gardener replied, "Not at all. I am Joshu. That's my best disciple."*

When you see a great guru, you might think the guru's path has not yet achieved its end. A master does not behave this way. He is invisible. He is a normal, ordinary man who travels the path until the end.

The Wooden Buddha in the Temple Fire

A monk meditates in a temple. He falls sleeps and while he's sleeping, he knocks over a small candle that sets the wooden ornamentation on fire. When the monk awakens, the fire intensifies. Because the temple was built completely from stone, from floor to roof, the structure resists the fire, though it won't burn out until it has destroyed all the wooden ornaments.

Before fleeing the fire, the monk tries to save a great wooden Buddha. Despite being weak, he finds the miraculous strength to lift the statue that weighs more than a hundred kilograms. When he arrives at the door, he realizes that the wooden Buddha is twice as tall as the door, and twice as wide. In other words, it is impossible to get the Buddha through the opening. The walls are too solid to move or break. But the monk doesn't want his beloved Buddha to burn. What can he do to escape unscathed with his treasure?

How will the monk take out the Buddha? Japanese people ask strange questions. And to think that some have devoted more than twenty years to similar questions!

The answer is not a joke: The monk carries the Buddha on his back, opens the door, and walks through it.

Many Zen koans deal with this topic and send the same message. For example:

Imagine you are completely trapped inside a block of stone. How can you get out? You get out of the block by taking a step forward or to the side.

Another example:

> *A goose lays an egg inside a bottle. A little later, the egg breaks and a goose emerges. "How can this goose get out of the bottle?" the master asks his disciple. The monk goes away to meditate. Twenty years later he requests an interview with the master and tells him he has solved the koan.*
>
> *"How did you solve it?" asks the master.*
>
> *"The goose has come out of the bottle," replies the disciple.*

The story of the stone temple with its wooden ornaments and its flammable Buddha is a mental trick created by our brain. We have gathered a series of data in the form of a problem that needs to be solved, but we can't lose sight of the fact that all that data is a mental trick, pure invention. The exceedingly narrow door of this *koan* is no more real than the difficulties we create for ourselves. Both are creations of the spirit. They are false.

We are the ones who set this limit of the small door. It's up to us (insofar as this door has the same nature as the Buddha and of the rest of the story) to solve the problem by ourselves and immediately.

There are many people who carry the weight of their lives and see themselves in trouble. They are comparable to this monk who gets stuck in a narrow doorway. They say, "Help me get out, I'm trapped."

"Get out!"

"I can't concentrate, what shall I do?"

"Concentrate!"

"I'm a coward."
  "Be courageous!"

"I'm weak."
  "Be strong!"

"I have no faith."
  "Believe! Seek step-by-step, and have faith."

I myself faced a mountain of invented problems. When I tried to overcome them, I stumbled upon my own shortcomings. My mind was stuck on principles that limited me and prevented me from going forward. My family story was the incubator of my limitations. Before I was born, and even before I was conceived, I had already been programmed to create a narrow door that would keep me trapped.

In general, we all experience difficult and oftentimes terribly painful problems that are nothing but the fruit of the imagination—creations of the mind.

First, the wooden Buddha doesn't exist. That's why we shouldn't carry it on our shoulders. Why do we carry such a burden?

Second, we fall asleep. Why do we fall asleep?

Third, the fire doesn't exist. And yet we make it real and it ends up setting us ablaze. Why do we get burned? We ourselves create the fire that destroys us. Why do we want to fall into this drama?

Fourth, the narrow door doesn't exist. We are trapped because of it, although we could pass through it at any time.

Water

Master U-Tsu, in the midst of meditating, was interrupted by a disciple who was eager to hear his teachings. U-Tsu scrutinized his disciple and then drew on the ground an ideogram that meant "water." He looked to his disciple, to see whether he had understood the sense of his gesture, but the latter's face showed only total incomprehension.

The master is meditating. To him, meditating means making real something that is real inside him.

Whatever he does, he does not do it for an audience—parents, family, society, and so on—but because he feels the need to do it. It's beyond all morality. He is what he is. He seeks nobody's love or blessing. He meditates because he believes in it. He believes in himself. He has liberated himself.

Perhaps his parents didn't condition him, as most parents do, to see the world as they do. They say, "If you want my love, see the world as I do, be as I want you to be." Nor has he experienced the need to limit himself, as we do when we are in a relationship. We say, in effect, "Put blinders on your eyes, look neither right nor left, but only at me."

Master U-Tsu is free to do whatever he wants. He focuses. He meditates.

The disciple comes, thirsty for knowledge. U-Tsu draws a circle, rather tight, and draws the symbol for water inside it, as if it were a cup full of water. The master gives him, thus, a concept. But then, how do you drink a concept? Things are done, lived. The words that are given to us are nothing but words. The word "water" does not quench our thirst.

The master has no knowledge to offer. He confronts his disciple with his question.

"You ask me for a concept. Do you want me to talk to you, to explain you to you? Instead of asking for explanations, be. If you are thirsty, drink water, not my concepts. I can teach you to learn, but I cannot give you your self, what you are."

What Is Buddha?*

A bonzo (Zen novice) asked his master,
    "What is Buddha?"
"And who are you?" was the master's response.
"I? I am myself."
"Do you know that 'I,' yes or no?"
"Of course I do!"
Lifting a fly chaser in front of the bonzo, the
    master asked, "Do you see this?"
"Obviously."
Then the master stood up, and as he was
    leaving the room, he concluded,
"I have nothing to say."

Buddha is a spiritual state, a state of awakening, of total awareness beyond the intellect.

"What is Buddha?" The bonzo's question is stupid. He tries to find a rational answer where the intellect has no place.

The master immediately gives him a solution. Instead of giving him a lecture on the ego, the I, and so on, he asks the bonzo, "Who are you?" In other words, "Who are you, the you who wants to know what that state of perfection is? Who do you think you are?"

We are usually taught to diminish ourselves. How can we be Buddha? Who are we? We have better things to do than look for a definition of Buddha. We know who we are, and knowing our deep value is more useful.

---

*Koan taken from *Au coeur du zen,* by Taiken Jyoji.

The bonzo answers, "I am myself." But here again his intervention is stupid. The "I" he describes is an everyday I, limited, the I of daily life, cultivated since his childhood. It expresses the obstructions and limitations he's integrated from his education.

By saying, "I am myself," the bonzo expresses how natural it is for him to perceive himself as a limited man who sees Buddha beyond him.

This answer annoys the master, who insists, "But do you know that 'I,' yes or no?" His question is clear: "Do you know that 'I' of whom you speak? Do you tolerate your personality or do you know it?" We all have to answer these questions. Do we bear what happens to us? Are we the storm or are we the blue sky in which the storm wreaks havoc? In this blue sky storms appear and disappear, while the sky remains unchanged.

I worked with a couple at a time when they were undergoing a period of crisis. I asked the woman, "Are you angry because of his bad behavior? Then face that anger and let it out. Don't hold on to it. It's all drama. Put aside your sorrows and let everything positive and essential blossom in your relationship."

After a while, the woman said to her partner, "You hurt me, but I love you. Yet I'm afraid to love you because I know that if you keep treating me as you do, you will break my heart."

I told her, "Let him be. Offer your heart to be broken. But don't offer it as a masochistic victim; know instead that behind the sorrow there is absolute peace. If you work this way, your awareness will never be shattered."

She thought about these words and then turned to her partner and said, "Even if you break my heart, I love you."

He broke out in tears and in less than three minutes, their relationship was repaired.

> *"Do you know that 'I,' yes or no?"*
> *"Of course!"*
> *The master then lifts an object and says,*
> *"Do you see this?"*

The bonzo answers, "Obviously," but he doesn't understand. This is why the master ends the conversation.

We have to see Buddha. We have to see him in ourselves as we see a fly chaser. If I don't see him, how am I going to know him? When I meditate, I meditate to see what I am. We are all Buddha. It's difficult to make a novice understand this.

Back to the World

A Buddhist monk asked Kejon, "How does an enlightened being come back to the world after meditating?"

Kejon answered, "A broken mirror does not reflect anything anymore. Fallen leaves never go back to their old branches."

I once conducted a seminar where everybody entered a trance state of deep meditation. At the end someone said to me, "What we have experienced is amazing. But now, once we leave this place, how are we going to be able to live in the world?"

Another time I lectured on a fascinating Kabbalistic book and someone asked,

"This is lovely, but what happens when we are in the outside world?"

This kind of question reveals that whoever formulates it has learned nothing. At the same time it means, "Your teachings are absolutely useless. They haven't help me solve anything. With you I advance a little bit, but as soon as I leave this place, the world erases everything, because it is not as you say it is. What can be done about it?"

When Kejon says, "When a mirror is broken, it doesn't reflect anything anymore; when leaves fall, they don't go back to their branches," he means, "You have to ask yourself that question. Stop worrying about tomorrow. Live the experience and then you will see. If you are profoundly enlightened, go into the world and see what happens. Once that mirror is broken, it doesn't reflect anything anymore. Once the ego is broken, it disappears. Once leaves have fallen, they don't go back to their branches; they are on the ground, in their proper place. When we experience change, this change gives us our place in the world."

Learning requires three conditions: the first is wanting to acquire knowledge, the second is knowing it is possible to do so, and the third is accepting the change that such knowledge provokes.

People stumble with this last point. They do whatever they can to change, but when change comes they worry, "What will happen when I go back into the world?"

"Listen, do your work! Meditate. Find yourself. Then go to the world and you will see. Don't tell me, 'Yes, but . . .'" Do what you need to do. Seek. Live. Achieve self-realization. Don't put obstacles in your path to self-realization under the pretext that the world doesn't contain the beauty you have inside you. Let your inner beauty blossom and be fulfilled without asking what will happen next or how the world will react.

Each of us has a place in this world. There is, of course, a place for the mad and the sadistic, but there is also a place for people who have worked on themselves. There is a place for positive people, for couples who work on creating their own divinity, for all those who do not accept negativity. Knowing this, what place will you choose?

I would rather live and meditate on a flower than on a carcass. That's what the Madman of the tarot of Marseille does. When we study this card, we can see that he walks on wonderful flowers. He goes from one pristine place to another and finds self-realization.

If the world were truly—really truly—imperfect, we wouldn't be able to compare it to anything. It would be perfect then. For imperfection to exist, there needs to be some small islands of perfection. They serve as reference.

Instead of going from imperfection to imperfection and dishonor to dishonor, look for the flaw in the system, the spaces of perfection, and don't go ahead without benefiting from them. This is how you will find your own happiness.

Infinity

To the fish in the water, the ocean is infinite.
To the bird in the sky, the sky is infinite.

The bird and the fish must be in their elements for them to be infinite. The bird drowns in water, and the fish asphyxiates in the air.

Is Buddha in the Dog?

One of Joshu's disciples asked him, "If the spirit of Buddha is in everything, is it also in the dog?"

As his only answer, Joshu barked.

Seizing the Sky

Joshu asked one of his disciples, "Can you seize the sky?"

Having seen Joshu bark in answer to the question about the dog, the disciple pretended to grab the sky with his hands. Joshu took him by the nose and squeezed it. The disciple released himself forcefully, and as he rubbed his hurting nose, Joshu said, "I just seized the sky."

The Master's Bones

One day Chan the monk said to his friend Lin, another monk, "If you want to know the master's teachings, ask him what enlightenment is."

Lin went to the master, and when he presented his question, the wise old man answered by giving him a sound thrashing.

Lin then ran out to tell Chan about his adventure. Chan was astonished by the answer and entreated Lin to repeat the question. Lin went again to the master's presence, posed the question again, and received another good thrashing.

When Chan learned that Lin had received the same

answer, he was again astonished and asked Lin whether he had understood the answer. Lin's eyes widened in surprise. What was there to understand? Chan advised him a third time to go in to the master's presence, and that's how Lin received a third thrashing.

Heartbroken, Lin left the monastery and began looking for a new master. In another province he found another master with a great reputation. He told him how he had been battered each time he had asked the question. The wise old man was immediately receptive and compassionate.

"Ask me your question right now," he proposed.

"Master, what is enlightenment?"

As the only answer, Lin received a sound thrashing. Flabbergasted, and without understanding anything, Lin went back to his old monastery. He went to see Chan and told him his latest mishap.

"I don't understand anything!" he said.

"Of course you have understood it perfectly," said Chan.

"Where is the master?" asked Lin.

"He has passed away," Chan responded.

This news threw Lin into profound distress from which he emerged with a new and sudden understanding. He took a shovel and walked firmly toward the graveyard, saying,

"I am going to unearth my master's bones to follow his teachings."

The Master's Death

A master was in agony. A disciple approached the dying man and begged,

"Tell me your last words! Entrust me with your spiritual will!"

"I don't want to die," replied the master. "That is my spiritual will. I don't want to die."

In the "Is Buddha in the Dog?" koan, the master, by barking, wants to express, "Penetrate the dog's nature. To know a thing, become that thing. Perceive it from within your being."

Become the beloved being! To get to know it, perceive it from within your being. This perception is not just mental. To understand the dog, you need to become one with the dog's nature. You really need to be him.

In the koan "Seizing the Sky," the disciple pretends to seize the sky and the master sees that it's nothing but an intellectual game. In the end the disciple has no sky in his hands. He has only ideals, illusions. He seeks an enlightenment that is not his, one that doesn't exist.

In the koan "The Master's Bones," the master thrashes his disciple many times so that his student will lose the sense of the duality of pain. When pain dominates us, it's no longer time for theories and insights on God and Buddha. Being completely immersed in pain is being enlightened, because being enlightened is living exactly what you are living at that moment—entering deeply into yourself. It implies being aware of everything you feel in the present moment.

When the disciple whose nose is squeezed by Joshu complains that it hurts him, Joshu responds, "I have seized the sky." In other words, "I have seized nonduality. I have seized your *self* just as it is."

A disciple asked Buddha, "How do I have faith?"

In answer, Buddha submerged his student's head in water and kept it there until the disciple was about to drown. When he was finally able to free himself, the disciple took a breath with the full force of his lungs.

"Did you need to breathe?"

"Yes," answered the disciple, still gasping.

"Well then, that is faith," concluded Buddha.

When the disciple tried to obtain a definition of enlightenment (or of faith), the master didn't hit him to punish him. Enlightenment is not superficial.

An intellectual went to a monastery to meet with an old monk who had a reputation as a wise man. He wished to discuss Buddha's nature with him, but the old man said,

"I need to go to the kitchen to prepare some mushrooms."

The intellectual took offense. "But why? You are one of the greatest spirits in Zen and you want to prepare mushrooms? Leave those chores to your disciples."

The old man got up, and as he was leaving the room, he replied, "You have understood nothing about the path. I am going to prepare the mushrooms myself."

Insisting on preparing the mushrooms himself, the old monk meant that the path did not consist of having theories, talking, or speculating about truth. He meant that truth is akin to being a fish in the ocean or a bird in the sky. It is surrendering fully and absolutely to yourself.

In the koan "The Master's Bones," the monk who

receives the thrashings feels great pain when he learns about his instructor's death, and it is then that he understands this reality. Through his pain he feels alive; he feels that he is. He understands who he is and that the master has hit him to take him to his truth through pain. At that moment he understands that he had a great master and he takes a shovel to unearth his bones, which are his current reality.

What is his master going to teach him now? He is going to show him what he is—a pile of bones. The disciple is entering into contact with that reality and accepting it. He is accepting what he is ("I am what I am") and he will learn.

Accepting yourself just as you are is communicating with yourself. It is using the intellect in what concerns the intellect—no more, no less. It is living what is physical in what is physical, what is emotional in what is emotional, what is sexual in what is sexual. And the union of these four egos is the union of these four egos.

To begin with, we ought to perceive ourselves just as we are. We must not tell stories to ourselves. We need to find ourselves.

When are we infinite? When our intellect perceives itself fully. Our hearts are infinite, love is infinite, and every instant is infinite. Our bodies are infinite.

In this complete reality no game is played. We stop lying to ourselves. We do not flee when we see the dark side of our sexuality. We also revise all our old concepts. And to the extent to which love passes through us, to the extent to which we become channels, we clear up our emotional life. We make our hearts infinite.

In the koan "The Master's Death," as the master was

dying a part of him rejected death, and he expressed that. He did not try to utter a phrase for posterity. In the immensity of his spirit, he could perceive the human cry that he carried within him.

Acknowledging our impulses. Being honest, not trying to bury ourselves. These koans are clear. We have to situate ourselves in our own reality.

Two Monks and a Nightingale

*In the monastery of Nansen, Enju, the gardener, was having a
discussion with Tenza, the cook. Suddenly, in the midst of the
conversation, a nightingale started to sing, and the two monks
interrupted their conversation to listen to her song. When the
bird became silent, the gardener—one of whose hands was
made of wood—used his real finger to tap a rhythm on his
artificial hand, and suddenly the bird trilled once again. The
two monks heard her again. When the nightingale became
silent for the second time, Enju again tapped a rhythm on the
wood of his hand, but the bird was silent.*

Enju asked the cook, "Do you understand?"

"No, I don't," replied Tenza, confused.

*Enju then tapped his hand with cadence. Tenza smiled
and the two men went their separate ways.*

Enju and Tenza live in a monastery. Becoming a monk means
wearing a uniform. The ego is left aside and one enters the
monastery aiming to find oneself. We stop seeking light in
the exterior in order to seek it within ourselves.

These two monks perform spiritual work on themselves,
and thus they analyze whatever happens to them as a form of
work. It can be said that they are sincere because this story
takes place at a time when masters have the right to make life-
and-death decisions for their disciples. Enju and Tenza com-
mitted their lives by becoming monks.

Who are they? Kings, business moguls, artists, fools? We
don't know. For them, appearances have disappeared. With

their uniform, they have given up on appearances and are seeking the state of being.

One is a cook and the other a gardener, which are not the most humble functions in the monastery. Generally the position of cook is the most important after that of master. Manual chores are not considered inferior. When working in the kitchen, one works on the substance of life. Truth is found in the kitchen, so a cook must be extremely conscious. The story of the cook who swallowed the serpent found in the soup illustrates this point.

The gardener also has an important role because he works with nature, the soil, and the seasons. Cook and gardener are thus among the most important posts, despite being humble ones. They know what to eat in order to meditate well.

Eating well is very important when you follow a spiritual path. You can't continue if you ingest rotten food. I am not in favor of a pure vegetarian diet (Christ himself was not vegetarian); however, I think it is good to considerably limit our meat consumption and not eat more than the body needs.

A friend of mine used so much cocaine that it affected his liver. He went to China to see a master of Taoist medicine and was ordered to eat pork to heal his liver. Meat can be a remedy, so it's not good to be too opposed to it. However, consciousness cannot be acquired without deep reflection on our own eating habits, making adjustments whenever necessary.

We may overindulge at times, but we then control ourselves and go back to a more moderate diet. There is a *mudra* that illustrates this situation quite well: "If the animal leaves the flock, I take it back to the flock. If it leaves again, I take it back again."

Spiritual work follows this principle, too. What is essential is to not be perfect. What is essential is having an internal mandate to get back on track whenever you have gone astray.

I know people who, from the moment they commit a "tiny sin," do nothing but fail again and again. They say, "Since I failed once, I am lost. I'm rotten, for all I know; I'm lost in the river."

Now you can see the beauty of these two monks, the gardener and the cook. Their beauty is superior to that of many great philosophers.

While they talk, a nightingale starts singing. I can't imagine the philosophers Jean-Paul Sartre or Gilles Deleuze stopping a conversation because a bird is singing. However, these two men are so sensitive that they become silent. They both are respectful of nature; they recognize its beauty and listen to its message.

If I am capable of recognizing the beauty of nature, I am capable of recognizing the beauty of my own nature. Otherwise, I am necessarily closing my eyes to my own beauty. To recognize nature, we need to put ego aside and stop struggling in the belief that the world revolves around us.

The gardener who responds to the bird's song has a wooden hand. At a symbolic level, this is a marvelous detail. How did he lose his hand? He may have sacrificed it, just as Bodhidharma's first disciple did in China.

When Bodhidharma arrived in China he stood up against a wall and refused to speak to anyone. A Chinese warrior wanted to become his disciple, but Bodhidharma ignored him. The man waited in vain for the master to agree to accept him. Days and months passed without Bodhidharma speaking to him. Then—according to the legend—the warrior cut off his arm and threw it at Bodhidharma's feet, saying, "If you don't turn around, I will cut off my head." In other words, "Learning is essential to me."

A man told me, "I want to become an artist." Then become it! If art is essential to you, you'll have to make some sacrifices.

A woman once told me, "I love a man. I want to be in a relationship with him, but he is not very enthusiastic. He feels no desire for me."

"If you really love him, whether he loves you or not has no importance. Become a champion. Arouse him. Make him go crazy. Caress him with incredible wisdom. Dedicate yourself to the project. His lack of desire is not a problem. Do not get fixated on that! Get into the awakening of the other person's desire, just as a wise man would do it. From that moment on, your doubts will go away and he will love you, but for that to happen, you need to forget about your demand for love. Stop wanting to be loved! Be active! If you blow at the embers, the flame will spark again. However, if you wait for the ashes to warm you . . .

"The man you love has a serious problem with his mother. You can't win him through either the heart or the intellect. That leaves your body and your sexuality. Use those! Initiate him.

"In a relationship with a man, you can be his mother, his wife, his sister, his daughter, or his prostitute, and you can also be his initiator. You have to stop playing the role of the good girl asking for daddy's love. Forget your problems and become his initiator. There are techniques for it. Learn them."

Men also need to learn techniques.

Nothing is achieved without sacrifice. Bodhidharma's disciple offered his arm. The gardener's wooden hand indicates he is a man who has sacrificed part of himself.

The major sacrifice is in offering the ego—the gift of self. We enter deeply into sacrifice and the ego gives way to the higher self.

That is what Enju and Tenza are deliberating. What do you expect them to discuss? Two monks in a monastery, isolated from the world, cannot chatter like two silly teenagers. They exchange important information on meditation techniques. They talk about spiritual work.

They suddenly abandon their exchange because reality— the truth—emerges. Then, not for any specific effect, the gardener uses a natural element—wood—because he knows the bird will recognize this sound. He doesn't just call the nightingale in a random way. He communicates with the creature by creating a sound that resonates with the natural world.

The bird understands this echo that the gardener sends and resumes singing. It is not the gardener who expresses himself, it's his wood—that is to say, his essential nature. He knows how to exclude himself and put himself inside the bird's experience. The nightingale must feel a resonance and trills back to him.

When the nightingale becomes silent the second time, the gardener again taps the wood to illustrate something to his companion.

Because the bird follows its nature, it doesn't hold on to anything. For the bird it's not a matter of singing in duet with the first gardener who arrives. The winged creature is free, and when inspired to sing, it sings. But nature is not repetitive, so the second tapping brings a different response. Repetition is artificial. The bird doesn't engage in the game or understand custom but flies off to live life. The bird is free and can follow whatever whim occurs. That is what the gardener wants to tell the cook when he asks him whether he has understood.

How does the cook respond? He could say, "Yes, I understand this fundamental philosophical problem. The song of this bird speaks to us of the absence and non-absence between the being and the non-being in the dual reality, and so on." He could say many different things.

> *A warrior showed up at the house of a great master in hopes of becoming his disciple. He opened the door and the master, seeing him at the entrance for the first time, drew a circle in the air and received the warrior by asking him what that meant.*
>
> *"Master," replied the hopeful future disciple, "I have just arrived and you are already drawing mysterious signs in the air . . . it's too soon. I don't understand what it means."*
>
> *"Come in and shut the door," replied the master. "You can be my disciple."*

The master accepted this new disciple because he acted naturally. He didn't lie. He didn't respond, "It's a wonderful circle that symbolizes perfection. You will teach me perfection." He expressed precisely his lack of understanding, which indicated that he was open to receiving the truth. In order to enter into truth, it is essential to recognize and accept that you don't already know it.

This is why the cook humbly says that he does not understand. He is not ashamed to say that he knows less than his companion. He speaks with his nature.

The gardener responds as the nightingale has responded. For him, the sincere word of a human being is comparable to the song of a bird. Making the wood "sing" for the last time means, "You are sincere. Like the bird, you speak with your original nature. It is wonderful when the bird is the bird, when you are you with your unique sincerity, beauty, and goodness, when I am myself, when wood is wood, and a cloud is a cloud."

The cook sees that the gardener treats him in the same way he treats the nightingale. When it is sincere, the human voice is as beautiful as the song of a bird.

I will now tell you once again this story, which no longer holds any secrets.

A monastery usually has an impeccable garden. Everything is perfect. Pathways are flawless. Some dead leaves scattered here and there add a slight touch of disarray. It is the gardener himself who has shaken the trees to make the leaves fall. They symbolize disorder within order and they speak to us of the impossibility of human perfection.

The kitchen is cared for in the same way as the garden. When the cook peels and cuts vegetables, all his gestures are conscious. Nothing is automatic. He never repeats the same gesture twice, because repetition allows the devil to enter.

When they meet, the two monks greet each other and in their greeting express the happiness of saying good morning to one another. Their happiness is even more intense since their master tells them "Every day is a good day." The master doesn't differentiate between good and bad days, meaning that every day possesses particular intrinsic qualities and the whole universe exists only for the present moment, the "here and now." There is nothing more beautiful than the present moment, because it is unique. It will never be repeated. The ephemeral aspect of time grants it an incredible quality.

If I am aware that every second is a good second and every day is a good day, I am in a state of grace and acceptance.

These monks know all this when they say good morning to each other. Next, in the beauty of this day, a nightingale sings. This song is as beautiful as a star, as beautiful as the sun, the moon, and the sand. It is music that emerges in a good day, in the uniqueness of that moment. Never again will this bird sing the same way, just as these monks will never feel and talk to each other in the same way ever again.

It is in this moment that will never be repeated that the gardener taps a rhythm on his hand, which was carved from a tree he himself cultivated. This is why he's a gardener. He works with a hand that is a product of nature. He has sacrificed something, but everything we sacrifice is given back through other means in a just way.

Symbolically, it's very good for a gardener to have a wooden hand. The French collective unconscious says that those who have talent for gardening have a green hand (in English, a green thumb), which is considered a good hand.

Tapping on his hand, the gardener plays an instrument of nature. The bird perceives this natural aspect of sound. It is a sound that is produced not by men, but by the universe. It is a single note among nature's millions of notes. The nightingale pays homage to the gardener by resuming chanting.

The gardener then starts again, but the bird is no longer there. The nightingale is free, and it has flown away on impulse.

The gardener turns to his companion, asking, "Do you understand?" His question is ecstatic. He expects nothing, he seeks to prove nothing. He limits himself to asking, "Have you understood?" The cook, in the ecstasy of his own uniqueness, joins in the ecstatic happiness of the other. He says, "I don't understand, but I totally admire what you are." He intuitively feels that something happens, even though he does not understand it with his intellect.

The gardener again taps his wooden hand, expressing in another way, "You have understood. You have understood not with your intellect, but with your happiness."

The two men acknowledge each other. They are in a shared state of ecstasy.

The White Stone

A master is holding a bowl in his hands at the moment a disciple asks him this enigmatic question: "Master, how do we break the white stone in a pile of garbage?"

The master lets the bowl fall to the floor, and as it breaks in a thousand pieces he responds, "Like this."

The disciple asks an intellectual question. The white stone represents self-realization and personal purity, and the garbage pile represents the world—an unevolved world, of course.

"How can we throw our personal purity into this garbage pile that is the world?"

"Like this."

Letting the bowl fall, the master says, "We stop intellectualizing and surrender ourselves to the world. We believe there is a profound and real union between the world and us. Everything is world. Everything is consciousness."

The Heart of the Tree

Seppo said to his disciple Chosei, "Come here, take the ax. Instead of meditating, we are going to chop down trees to build a cabin."

Chosei accompanied his master to the woods of the monastery. As he was about to start chopping a tree, Seppo said to him, "Do not stop cutting until you reach the heart of the tree."

Without swinging a single stroke, Chosei replied, "I have already reached it."

"Perfect," Seppo responded. "Our Buddha has made a direct transmission from heart to heart. Nothing is written. Have you received the transmission?"

"Transmission received," said Chosei, and he threw down his ax.

Seppo picked it up and tapped his disciple's head with the handle. "Instead of meditating and working on spiritual pursuits inside the monastery, let's do some manual labor. Let's build something useful. However, when you cut the tree, don't stop until you reach its center."

What this means is, "When you start your work of spiritual transformation, don't stop until you have reached your center."

The astute disciple immediately understood the sense of the master's words and said, "I have already reached it," thus expressing that he had found his center.

The master accepted this affirmation. He added, "Buddha

has transmitted his teaching from heart to heart. Nothing is written. Have you received the transmission?"

"I have received it," replied his disciple, and by throwing away his ax, he clearly showed that for him the job was done. There is no need to spend hours and hours meditating, studying, searching, following the teachings of all the masters we meet, working on energy, practicing tantra, yoga, and so on. When we perceive that the transformation directly touches our heart, it's done.

Then the master hit him, communicating, "Even now you have fallen into a trap, because you believe there is such a transmission." When you work spiritually, nobody transmits anything to you. You simply find your center. As the philosopher Gurdjieff used to say, "Nobody can piss for you." You are the only one who can do it. If you find, you find. You can be helped, but this story of transmitting knowledge is just one more story that illustrates pitfalls of the ego.

The Visit of Master Tanka

When Master Tanka went to visit Master Echu, he found Huynen, Echu's disciple, asleep at the temple door. He woke him up and asked, "Is your master inside?"

Without looking at the visitor, Huynen sleepily replied, "My master doesn't want to see anybody."

"Your observation is profound," observed Tanka.

"Even if Buddha himself came, my master wouldn't receive him," added Huynen confidently.

Before leaving, Tanka concluded, "Your master will be proud of you."

When Echu was leaving the temple, Huynen recounted the conversation he'd had with Master Tanka. Echu then whacked him with a cane and threw him out of the temple.

This koan is part of the history of Zen. The encounter between Tanka and Echu's disciple may have actually taken place.

I will tell you this koan again using my own words. The story begins with a master. To be a master means being profoundly centered in oneself.

Most people are incapable of entering their center. We are afraid to see our own emptiness. Even the beating of our hearts impresses us. Feeling our hearts, strengths, or energies makes us feel apprehensive. To enter into the depth of our inner being, we need to set aside sadness, pain, madness, death, and more.

A master faces himself, and in so doing, he faces up to the divine aspect that lies deep within the center of his being. This master accepts a disciple . . . he doesn't admire him and wish to take his place, but he wants him to learn to be himself. Anyone who introduces himself as a real master and tells you, "Come to me, I'm fantastic. You will be at my service your entire life and in exchange, I will take care of you," is not what he says. A real master does not say, "I am delighted because I will take care of all your worries, as well as your money and energies. The ego is something bad. Renounce yours and use mine, which is much better."

A master, Tanka, visits another master, Echu. What do two masters do when they meet? They enjoy a wonderful silence together. If they feel like communicating, they do, but whatever they say to each other, their exchange is serene and collaborative. They may sing or play. They meet to share a pleasant moment.

If a master abandons his temple to meet another master, it's because he is weary of his disciples. He wants to relax in the company of somebody who won't ask him anything, won't judge him, won't get involved in his private life, and will leave him alone. Only a master can offer such a quality relationship. A disciple, on the other hand, would be likely to make a hole in the bathroom wall to spy on his master.

If Master Tanka goes to visit Master Echu, it means the weather is pleasant—so pleasant that Echu's disciple is taking a nap. In times of good weather, the master doesn't sleep. He has a rendezvous with someone at his same spiritual level.

Meanwhile, the disciple has a wonderful mission to accomplish—he has to guard the door. Instead of fulfilling his task, he takes a nap. How can someone sleep at such a moment? In spiritual work, there is no room for complacency.

You cannot abandon yourself. A disciple who sleeps on the job remains outside himself, admiring his master.

When Tanka sees Huynen sleeping, his personal "data processor" examines him. He reaches the conclusion that Huynen falls asleep on his internal work just as he falls asleep in front of the temple.

He approaches him and asks, "Is your master inside?" Now we understand that he is asking, "Is he inside you? Is Echu your master or do you have your own inner master?"

Christ didn't cure the paralyzed man without first asking him whether that was his wish. The paralytic affirmed his will to be cured and only then could the miracle be performed. That means that the question was, "Do you have an inner master of your own? Do you have the cure within you?"

"If you have the cane, I'll give it to you. If you don't have it, I'll take it away from you," says the Zen tradition. And the Gospel says, "To him who has, will be given, and to him who has nothing, even that little he has will be taken away from him." In other words, "Do you have the cure within you? If you do, I will give it to you. If not, I'll take it away from you."

Huynen, asleep at the door, has no doubt that Tanka is asking him about Echu, who is inside the temple. He responds, "My master is inside, but he doesn't want to see anyone."

"Your observation is profound," notes the visitor.

This means that our inner master doesn't want to see our little personal flaws—the deformities of ego. He doesn't want to see our little depressed personality, our everlasting inner child from whom we refuse to grow up, our decadent intellect, our closed heart, our desire to destroy ourselves physically, and so on.

"My inner master doesn't want to see all our little imperfections" is a deep answer. However, when the disciple adds, "Even if Buddha came he would not receive him," it implies that this idiot is proud of having such a master, yet he is incapable of feeling proud of himself. Buddha doesn't come from anywhere; he is inside us.

Whatever our spiritual level may be, that of others is of no use to us. It is useful only to show us where we ourselves can go. The master teaches the path for everyone. He is not an exceptional being who possesses a treasure; he is an individual who works ceaselessly on himself. A perfectly common man who cuts back the rocks that contain his inner diamond . . . a diamond we, too, possess. Sarcastically, Tanka says to Echu's disciple, "Your master will be proud of you." Huynen feels delighted with the compliment. Don't study to gain a master's approval; you will be seeking again your parents' approval through a substitute. What is the point of getting the best grades in your theater classes, or in medicine, or in anything else if you're just going through the motions and don't like what you do? Don't do it only to meet your parents' expectations.

When I was a child, everything I did was to get my parents' approval and admiration. I did nothing but what I didn't want to do. My true self was forbidden to me; it was not part of their expectations. As an adult, I continue to feel guilty about everything I do when I am truly myself.

By forcing myself into the role of a "nice" person, I end up brooding. Just like that "very nice" guy on the news that everyone is buzzing about, who raped a five-year-old girl. He was, however, so sweet! How could such a nice person commit such an act? In fact, this person is a real "pressure cooker." People are like pressure cookers. They are wound tightly. In a restaurant, they never put their elbows on the table. They speak without raising their voices and have excellent manners . . . but one day comes the rape, the crime, the suicide, or something else. Being nice, trying to be loved, transforms us into pressure cookers. We're forbidden to talk, to understand, to see, to touch . . . everything is forbidden.

The disciple adopts an attitude of admiration in front of his master. When the master comes, he proudly recounts his conversation with Tanka, seeking his approval, but Echu throws him out of the temple. It's his way of saying, "Stop living for my sake. You have understood nothing. I don't need you to be what I am. If you are my disciple, it's only to get to yourself."

Mokugen's Smile

Mokugen's master never smiled in his entire life. He remained always aloof. He did his work and consecrated himself to his temple. He was always intensely present. At the moment of his death, knowing he was going to die, he gathered his disciples and said,

"Tell me what you have learned from Zen. I will give my robes and bowl to the monk who tells me what Zen really is. He will become the new director of this monastery."

The disciples surrounding him started to philosophize but could come up with nothing, since there's nothing to be said about Zen. A disciple approached Mokugen's bed. He took a bowl of medicine and gently brought it to the ailing man's lips. Sarcastically, Mokugen said, "Hah! Is this all you have learned about Zen?" The disciple stared at his master, put the bowl back in its place, and calmly looked up again. It was then that Mokugen smiled for the first time in his life and said, "You rascal! I give you my robes and my bowl. The monastery is yours."

And he died happy.

This koan tells through very simple means a deep story of love and devotion. All the disciples seek an intellectual definition of enlightenment. They don't know how to escape the intellect. In reality, the intellect can never offer truth. All the disciples are incapable of answering.

In contrast, one of them approaches the ailing man thinking to himself, "I couldn't care less about the robes, the bowl, and the management of the monastery. Master (and with this word "master" he expresses immeasurable love), you have been my father, my teacher; you are my refuge in this life. Knowing what Zen is has no importance for me. I would rather have you cured. Take your medicine and stay with us."

He brings the bowl close to the old man's lips. In this gesture Mokugen understands the immense love his disciple feels for him. He says to him, "Is this all you have learned about Zen?" What he means is, "You have learned to think death is a negative event. You think you are going to lose something. You feel you are being abandoned, that I am abandoning you. . . . Your state of mind does not correspond to an awakened spirit, since nothing comes and nothing goes—the present is one. If I am completely identified with life, I do not leave. I am here. I am life."

The disciple understands all this in his master's gaze and puts the bowl back in its place. He is communicating, "In that case, I understand. Don't worry about the monastery anymore. Die in peace. I'm here for the temple."

So then the master answers, "You rascal! You understood right away. Well done. Here are my robes and my bowl." We don't need words to understand each other. Love substitutes for words and allows instant understanding.

Submit!

"Master, I am afraid of dying. Can you help me solve that problem?"

"Yes, I can."

"Tell me what to do."

"Submit!"

Die so that you won't die. Dissolve your ego, your individual "I." Only the death of the individual exists. The whole of life never ends. To be eternal, puncture your ego.

At night, especially when my activity is intense and I can't fall asleep, I practice an exercise I like a lot. I say, "From now on, I will stop thinking."

I relax, and after a while, my thinking evaporates. So I add, "And now? Now, I surrender to nothingness. I am nothing."

I surrender to the nothingness for a while. It then occurs to me to think, "I am very happy. I've achieved it. . . . Enough! Stop being happy! If you are happy it means you're not in the nothingness. Agreed, I'm not happy."

I get into this idea, but I end up telling myself, "Don't be sad either. Abandon yourself to the situation. Enter into the nothingness. Accept it."

After a few seconds, I sleep profoundly. It seems as though we fall asleep in the moment in which we accept nothingness, because the intellect disappears. When you extinguish the intellect, you sleep; you enter the universe.

There's nothing more alive than a sleeping being. His intellect is completely absorbed in the universe. Entering into nothingness without falling asleep would be wonderful. Unfortunately, it hasn't yet been achieved.

To achieve what you want, do the job yourself. If you go to a true master so that he can give you wisdom and truth, you will realize that the master has only his own truth, and that he counts on you to find your own truth.

Open Hand, Closed Hand

A disciple complained to his master about how much his wife was spending. "Can you help me? My wife spends and I am going broke."

The wise man went to visit his disciple's wife. He reached his clenched fist toward the woman's face and said, "Imagine if my hand were to remain in this position day and night until the end of my life. What would you say?"

"I would say it has a malformation," replied the wife.

Satisfied with the answer, the wise man opened his hand entirely and asked, "And what would you say if it stayed like this day and night?"

"I would say that, too, is a malformation."

"If you understand this," concluded the wise man, "you understand how to be a good wife."

Let us say that a closed hand is a hand that retains and an open hand is a hand that gives. Giving all the time is as terrifying an attitude as constant avarice. When is a hand alive? When it moves between these two positions, giving or not giving depending on the circumstances.

In my opinion a human being shouldn't have fixed attitudes. A fixed behavior is comparable to a hand with a malformation. It denotes a problem—a monstrous deformity of the self. If we observe ourselves we can examine whether we always have the same behavior, if it is exactly the same all the time.

We all know people like that. In general, they're very

self-indulgent. For them, man is incapable of change. They can't imagine anything would be an improvement. If confronted with one of their peculiarities, they shrug and excuse themselves, saying, "I can't help it, this is how I am." And they make no effort to improve.

If they have only one arm, the right one, and therefore only one hand, and it is closed (as in the story), they can't pick their noses. What to do then? There's nothing left but to open the hand (what an effort!) to clean their noses, tolerating the discomfort. They are then accepting themselves as they are.

Cutting Off Buddha's Neck

Isan bumped into his master, Gyosan, in a monastery after a hundred-day meditation session. The master said, "I haven't seen you in recent months. What have you been doing?"

"I have been working on a piece of land and harvested a big load of millet."

"You haven't worked in vain," Gyosan observed.

"And what have you done, oh Master, during these last months?"

"At noon I ate frugally and at midnight I slept a few hours."

"I see you haven't been wasting your time either, Master."

"You should learn some self-respect," replied Gyosan.

A master is someone who devotes himself entirely to his disciple, before the latter can maintain on his own. He doesn't "work on" his disciple as if he were a sculpture. This would be the realm of Pygmalion, the sculptor who carved a statue and fell in love with it. The master does not give the disciple life but rather guides him constantly so that he will build it himself.

The master has nothing to give. His duty consists of directing his disciple's work. If the disciple doesn't do what he has to do, no master could be good enough to help him.

"Quit smoking!"

"I can't."

"Then I won't be your master."

"Quit drugs!"

"That's impossible for me."

"Since you chose me as a master, make an effort to achieve it. Start by doing this."

Gurdjieff ordered a man to quit smoking, and after seven years of effort, the man succeeded. When he told Gurdjieff, the latter took a pipe out of his coat, handed it to him, and said, "Now, smoke."

He advised the poet René Daumal not to make love for a year. On the other hand, he advised Luc Dietrich—another poet—to make love with a different woman each time.

A master—it is useless and futile to doubt him. The end is not the master, but oneself. Battatraya's *Advajuta Gita*, translated by Alexandra David-Neel, says, "Do not ask a boat for help in crossing a painted river." Don't pay attention to the master's flaws as long as he helps you cross your river.

In this koan we see a disciple who is very proud of his work. Gyosan asks him, "What have you been doing in the last months? How is your meditation going?" And the disciple responds, "I have been working on a piece of land. I have been working on myself. I've gathered a lot of millet; this is productive for me. I have nourished myself spiritually. I have made progress."

With this, Isan wanted to indicate to his master that he didn't need him anymore. "And you," he added "what have you done?" He ranked himself as equal to his master.

Facing such pretentiousness, Gyosan responded, "I have simply done what I have always done. At noon, I eat a little bit, and at midnight, I sleep a little bit." By saying, "You haven't been wasting your time either," Isan poked fun at Gyosan. In his mind, his master had fallen on his knees.

Instead of getting upset, Gyosan made a simple observation: "If you put me down, you put yourself down as well, since you chose me as your master. You are not showing self-respect. Be true to your values! Knowledge and enlightenment cannot be the object of competition. We are not evaluating our own merits or our respective powers. What matters is your own spiritual evolution."

When we say, "If you see Buddha, cut off his neck," we mean something else. It is not a joke or a lack of respect. I destroy an image fabricated by my mind so that Buddha can be made real inside me.

Koans

A Million Things

In anguish, Isan asked his master Gyosan, "What should we do if a million objects come toward us?"

"A green object is not yellow. A long thing is not short."

Satisfied with this exchange, Gyosan and Isan went their separate ways.

"Master, life makes me anxious. I feel drowned by its multiplicity. Millions of bits of information come in my direction. They all tempt me. I am overrun. It makes me feel desperate."

"Don't worry. Your perception can capture only one thing at a time. Therefore, it's useless to be anxious in advance. Live everything as it presents itself to you. When a green object presents itself, it is unique. It is not all objects. Accept it as it is and live it. There aren't a million instants to be lived; only the present instant exists. The rest will come after this. They are on their way to becoming the present instant, but if you remain calm, relaxed, without speculating or feeling too much anguish, one will follow another and your life will turn out very well."

77

The One-Pound Shirt

"Master, it is said that everything comes from the One, but where does the One come from?"

The master smiled and responded, "When I was in Osaka, I made myself a shirt that weighed one pound."

"Thank you, Master, I understand."

The disciple's question is a metaphysical one that has no answer. There are things to which we can give no answer. Some mental data are ambiguous. Cardinal directions, for instance, lack any tangible reality; they vary according to the place from which they are considered. At the North Pole, it is impossible to go north.

The master responds, "A one-pound shirt is too heavy. It would be torture to wear it. Stop asking questions that are impossible to answer. Stop working with your intellect in vain. Your question has no answer. Its foundations are ambiguous. Occupy yourself with real things.

"What is the One? It's you, it's me. It's my concentration in making a shirt. Come back to what is real. Take action. Do things with absolute concentration."

Break the Shape

"Master," says the disciple, "it has been said that he who purifies his spirit is able to see all. But can he see the shape of all things?"

"Shatter it in pieces," replies the master.

"How can we break it?"

"If you use force, it will fly into your face."

I found this fragment in an old compilation of Joshu's koans. Joshu was a master who lived 120 years ago.

In this koan the disciple asks whether someone who has purified his sight and is able to see everything can see shapes. I think that if he can see everything, he no longer sees shapes (the containers), because the content exceeds the shape. The master replies, "Shatter it into pieces." I assume he is speaking about the shape.

In this compilation, I also came across a little poem:

> *Wrapped in a million clouds*
> *I don't see these clouds.*
> *Lost in the sound of water flowing*
> *I can't hear the water flowing.*

With this poem, we now have the necessary material to interpret the koan.

Here we have a monk who thinks there are too many shapes in the world—too many imperfect, superficial things, and too many temptations. He is overwhelmed by their abundance.

I, who seek self-realization, ask myself, "If I saw everything, would I see all kinds of shapes, or only what is essential?

Would I see in others and in myself the incessant movement of the ego, or would I be capable of seeing our essential juncture, our Christ, our Buddha, our internal God?"

This monk is absorbed by the question, "How can I get to the essence? How can someone who has purified his sight see the unity? Is it really possible to see the unity? Can the essential be seen? Does shape exist?"

We could say that since he asks all these questions, the disciple hasn't resolved anything yet, which is not the case of the master he is addressing. The latter responds, "Shatter the world into pieces. Instead of trying to unify it, leave it as it is. If it is presented through a million facets, leave it with its million facets. Don't try to experience this unity."

This is what I advised a young graphic artist who complained about not being able to focus on anything (he was torn among multiple things): "Don't make any effort."

The monk replies to Joshu, "How do we accept the diversity of the world? How do we shatter it into pieces?"

"If you resort to force, it will hurt and destroy you," says Joshu.

Using force hurts and destroys, because searching for yourself doesn't mean opposing the world. In meditation, we do not oppose anything. Neither do we seek to obtain anything. We enter deeply into the spiritual and mental process that inhabits us. Meditating is being wrapped in clouds, lost in the sound of water, and getting to ourselves in the center of the diversity of the world. It is finding our essential self, the unity that we are. Our self is part of the unity.

And thus Joshu's answer is, "Stop feeling anxious while you seek your self. You want to find the truth at all cost.

Don't force things! Let things come, let things happen. Get inside your little jewel. Be what you are."

Jehova's essential answer is, "I am who I am."

This koan addresses many situations. Among the people who come to talk with me, some make great efforts to not be who they are, and to not accept the richness of their desires.

Usually the "ordinary" man (to use this terminology) is someone who hides his thoughts. He has been banned from thinking freely, and thus whenever thoughts come to his mind, he selects and censors some of them. He also selects and censors the images that come to his mind, the feelings that appear in his emotional life, the desires that arise from his sexuality, and the needs that his body expresses. He limits himself mentally, emotionally, sexually, and corporeally, erecting barriers that protect him from everything that is new and constantly inundating him. He appropriates these barriers that have been imposed on him.

This koan advises us to stop forcing ourselves into doing things and to accept whatever appears in ourselves, both the repugnant and the sublime.

We stay at the state of the common man for fear of seizing whatever is too low or too high in ourselves. We isolate ourselves in what is permitted and we reject all else, thinking it doesn't correspond to us. However, it all belongs to us, and it is what constitutes our richness.

Someone "ordinary" is someone who never changes throughout his life. Not changing is his major characteristic . . . unless he has an accident. The accident is his claim to fame, his grand adventure. He looks for it . . . a fire in his house, the death of a close relative, illness . . . these events plague his daily life. He has no other perspective.

Where Are You?

The disciple tells his master in confidence, "I am overwhelmed. I can't stop vacillating between two states—sometimes I drown, sometimes I float. When will I free myself from this world of suffering? When will I be free?"

The master doesn't respond. After a couple of minutes, the surprised disciple interrupts again.

"Master, am I not here, sitting in front of you, asking you a question?"

"Where are you now?" asks the master. "Floating or drowning?"

For the master, there is no doubt that here and now, in the present, we are self-realized. Self-realization is present.

If he comes back to the present with his master, the disciple shows he is self-realized. If he wonders if he is floating or drowning, he isn't living in the moment. In the end he understands he is neither drowning nor floating. He is a diamond next to another diamond, a Buddha beside another, a perfection beside another.

The difference between the two men lies in the fact that the master has made his perfection reality. The monk has not. In seeking it he thinks he will either drown or float. He creates enormous anxiety in order not to be fully present.

This is why the master doesn't reply to him. If the disciple tells him in confidence that he feels he is sometimes floating, sometimes drowning, it indicates that he isn't present in the moment, and in that moment nothing allows him to float or drown. There is no ocean, no water, no anguish, just peace.

The master doesn't reply to an absent disciple. The latter insists, "Master, I am talking to you!" The master says, "If you are talking to me, where are you?"

Let us let things arrive without feeling affected by them. They will come. We will be in the midst of them, but we will remain centered in the present moment. We will not get submerged in the clouds or in the sound of water. We will be here.

Becoming One with the Path

"Master, what is entailed in becoming one with the path?"

"Not being yourself."

"How can we not be ourselves?"

"You should be able to understand it through what I just told you."

"What does it mean to become one with the path?" In other words, how can you simultaneously be the path, wisdom, and yourself? Whoever poses this question is an intellectual who has experienced nothing. He has some beliefs, but he hasn't realized any. It's like an impotent lecturer speaking about orgasm.

"What does it mean to become one with the path?"

"It is not being one," replies Joshu.

That is, "Forget the intellect. Act! Dive headfirst into existence. Be yourself. Live your life."

The disciple adds, "And if we are not ourselves, what are we?" He hasn't understood anything. His seeking mechanism is prepackaged and doesn't allow him to give himself the essential answer.

Joshu responds, "You should be able to discover it through what I just told you. Instead of asking me questions, I advise you to stop your intellect, stop it and be aware of how you feel."

Here is a therapist's secret: When somebody comes to an appointment, full of problems, we make him sit facing us and we ask, "How do you feel?" He talks about his problems but doesn't go beyond speaking in anecdotes. At that point we help him refocus and ask once again, "How do you feel? Go deep into yourself and see how you feel." If he goes back to the anecdotes, we center him once again, as many times as necessary, until he manages to enter deeply into himself and feel the state he is in.

When he achieves this, we can pass to the next step. We ask him, "What do you desire?" We help him get into himself to discover what he really desires.

In short, throughout the entire session, we pay absolute attention to the person and help him discover how he deeply feels and what he deeply desires. That's it.

"Master, what does it mean to be oneself?"

"Not being oneself. Stop your intellect!"

"Master, what does it mean to stop the intellect?"

"Stop it!"

The Dog's Nature

The disciple asks Joshu, "Master, does the dog also have Buddha nature?"

"Mu."*

Why did Joshu respond "mu" to the monk? He didn't give him any answer. We don't know whether or not the dog has Buddha nature, and that's that.

This koan is one of the most famous ones. It's like the entrance door to Zen Buddhism. Whoever solves it reaches the state of enlightenment.

The question the monk is formulating is not essential. Having or not having (Buddha nature) isn't important.

What is Buddha nature?
What is Buddha?
What are we talking about?

Joshu responds to his disciple, "Stop your intellectual musings! Mu." This means, "Build the vacuum. Concentrate and cease your mental striving."

---

*In Japanese, *mu* means "nothing."

Nansen's Arrow

When Joshu arrived at a master's house, he was greeted with
the following words:
   "Here comes Nansen's arrow."
   "Look at the arrow," Joshu observed.
   "You missed!" replied the master.
   "It's right on target," replied Joshu.

In this koan, Joshu—who was Nansen's disciple before—goes
to see a master. This master is filled with knowledge, full of
teachings to transmit. Joshu has no knowledge. He is himself.

Seeing Joshu, this master says, "Here comes Nansen's
arrow. This guru is sending one of his disciples to challenge
me."

"Look at the arrow" is a wonderful response. It means,
"Don't look at Nansen's arrow. Look at who I am. Get out
of your own head, out of your preconceived ideas, out of
your judgment. Don't see Nansen through me. Stop thinking
about knowledge in terms of competition. If someone presents himself to you, do not judge him. See him as he is. See
your guest's essence."

When he says, "Look at the arrow," Joshu pushes the
arrow deep into the master's heart. The master defends himself, saying, "You missed." In other words, "You've missed the
target." And Joshu replies, "It's right on target."

Joshu is so pure that he does not enter into the other master's competitive game. He says to him, "Look at the arrow.
Look at me."

"You missed it! You weren't able to enter into my essence."

"I hit right on target because I don't want to enter into your essence. I have no intention of being your master, nor do I seek your approval. I haven't come here to challenge you or to teach you a lesson. I am myself, you are yourself. If we are on the same vibration, all the better. I do not want to influence you because I believe that when we respect other people's self-realization, we don't care about being at a higher spiritual level."

Joshu and the Birds

Joshu was a hermit who lived in the mountains and pursued enlightenment. Birds used to come to bestow flowers at his feet. Later he went to work beside a real master, Doshin. He became enlightened, and from then on, birds never again came to put flowers at his feet.

This is the necessary introduction to the next koan.

"Before Joshu worked with Doshin, birds dropped flowers at his feet. Why did they stop doing so?" asked the disciple.

Joshu answered, "To be attached to the pleasures of the world. Not to be attached to the pleasures of the world."

"When the disciple made efforts to reach the state of enlightenment, birds offered flowers. Why, Master? Why did they stop doing so when he became enlightened?"

Joshu did not answer. "Being or not being attached to material things, to the pleasures of the world." He used two phrases: "Being attached. Not being attached."

When this man was pursuing enlightenment, he was still attached to the world. He was putting so much effort into his pursuit that his life was full of wonders. He was doing the impossible to find something, without knowing what he was seeking. This effort was attracting birds, and they bestowed flowers at his feet.

Likewise, many gurus gather at their feet numerous women bedecked with flower necklaces who revere them a thousand times. When they reach true self-realization, they no longer need all that spectacle. They are no longer interested in applause and pompous bows. They become invisible.

A true master is invisible. No need for him to either disguise himself or be counted on the census. Reality is what is. When we present ourselves as saints, we deceive ourselves. We have achieved nothing. The temptation of prophesying, of wanting to be a master, of wanting to teach others, is great. It's an incredible temptation.

The Monk, the Bridge, and the River

The monk walks on the bridge. The river flows under the bridge.

The monk does not walk over the bridge. The river doesn't flow under the bridge.

"The monk walks on the bridge."

"Yes."

"Water flows under the bridge."

"Yes."

"The monk does not walk on the bridge."

"No."

"The river does not flow under the bridge."

"No."

If I say the monk walks on the bridge, I mean he walks over it; if I say he does not walk on the bridge, he does not walk over it. The same happens with the water that flows under the bridge. When I say it flows, it flows; when I say it doesn't flow, it doesn't. I don't need to link the two phrases together. They are two completely different situations. When two phrases come one after the other, we don't need to link them to draw a conclusion.

Who said it should be done? It is our thinking. It looks for results where none are necessary.

The Spirit at the Center

"Master, is the spirit directly at the center?"

"Stop! Stop! No need to explain it. My teachings are subtle and difficult to understand."

"Master, what does it mean to carry our spirit directly to the center?"

"Stop! Stop!"

By saying "Stop!" Joshu means, "Stop asking, stop thinking, If you want to go directly to the center, you don't need directions or explanations."

"My teachings are subtle." They aren't based on words or concepts.

"They are difficult to understand." Nothing is understood with the brain. Be yourself. Going directly to the center is going directly to your inner self. Stop trying to educate yourself the way scholars do. Knowing a lot of useless concepts is one thing. Knowing your own internal answer is something different.

Falling into the Well

"All clear, a tiny stain, what is it?"
"It's falling into the well."
"But where is the mistake?"
"You pushed the man into the well."

A poem says, "A grain of sand in the blue sky at noon stains the entire sky." If a perfect, enlightened person has the slightest dark desire, it means he is not yet perfect, unless he recognizes that desire and purifies it.

"Perfectly clear, a tiny stain, what is it?" The disciple posing this question doesn't know the answer. He has never experienced the immense joy of seeing himself as a living being. He asks, "What does it mean to live without the slightest stain?" Joshu replies, "Falling into the well."

With this answer Joshu is saying to him, "Your intellect is betraying you. Instead of making real all the questions you ask, instead of opening up like a flower, you seek conceptual answers. You have thus fallen into a well; you have fallen into the darkness of dry intellect."

The disciple insists, "Where is the mistake?"

"You pushed the man into the well." You have pushed your entire humanity into the well of intellectual inquiry. You want to obtain ready-made answers for some problems.

Someone consulted me to see whether or not she should have a child. I find it strange when people ask me these kinds of things. It's the person herself who should find the answer to this question. She should leave aside the intellectual question, "Should I? Should I not?" Let her enter into herself and not into the well of desire.

Once you know what you want, you can then decide whether or not to do it.

The Sleeping Attendant

Tangen was an attendant at Master Echu's house. One night his master called him. Tangen stood up, went to Echu's room, and said through the door, "I'm here, Master. What do you want?"

He didn't get any answer. Echu's room remained drowned in silence. Thinking that he might have been mistaken, Tangen went back to bed.

Some minutes later, as he was falling asleep, he heard his master loudly calling him, "Oh, attendant!"

He went again to the door of his master's room and asked, "Yes, Master, what can I do for you?"

As had happened the first time, he didn't receive any answer. He insisted a little, but it was in vain. Perplexed, he went back to his room. Just as he was lying down, he heard his master calling him, "Oh, attendant!"

Back at Echu's doorstep, he answered, "Master, you have called me three times, here I am!"

"Come in."

Tangen entered the room. Echu, who was seated on his bed, looked at him and said, "You have been studying with me for some time and you haven't achieved the state of enlightenment. I felt ashamed. I was sure I was being a bad teacher. Now I know I wasn't the one to blame. I thought I owed you an apology, but it's you who owes me one."

When we hear such a story, we tend to be astonished. We think, "He has taken all this time to tell me this. What does it even mean?"

Let us revisit this koan.

In this story there is a master—a meditation master, a healing master—a master. I, as his disciple, have chosen him. If I have chosen him, I have to trust him. He must find the method, but I must follow him.

I have become his attendant. I assist him. I am constantly with him throughout the day. At night, I sleep in the room next to his. He calls me in the middle of the night. I wake up saying, "What is it? What can I do for you?"

I offer him my services. He does not answer. After a while I go back to my room, but shortly afterward he calls me again. I run to his door, but I'm greeted with only silence. He doesn't say anything else. I go back to my room. He calls a third time. I go back to him the third time, he invites me in, and then he censures me. He tells me he was feeling bad because of me, that he'd thought he was responsible for my not having achieved the state of enlightenment, and that he'd thought he was a bad teacher. But now he realizes it's I who owe him an apology, and not he who owes me one. I don't understand . . . anything at all!

The first time I read this story I wondered what it meant, and I felt sorry for the poor disciple. He was there, ready to be called for service. Each time he was summoned, he showed up immediately. Why was this old man criticizing him?

However, seen from a different point of view, this story can acquire a very different sense.

"Oh, attendant, remember who you are. Remember it." When I am fully asleep and completely distracted, I remember about myself.

I'm smoking marijuana . . . "Oh, remember who you are."

I am caught up in seduction . . . "Oh, don't lose your mind. Remember who you are."

I have chosen a master to wake me up, to help me reach a higher spiritual level, and now I speculate about him. I superimpose my father's image onto his and I attack him.

"Attendant, stop this game. We are here, here and now. There's nothing more beautiful than spiritual work. Reaching your full potential. Remember who you are."

"Attendant, you are training to participate as an intern. You haven't come here to seduce the participants. Stop this game! You have come here to awaken, to find yourself."

When Tangen hears Echu's call, he thinks the latter needs him. However, Echu doesn't need anything. He only tries to give Tangen an example. He says to him, "Direct yourself. Enter into yourself. Remember yourself."

Tangen doesn't understand the message. He offers his services. Echu says, "He doesn't listen well." He doesn't reply, intending to make him understand, "I don't need you. It's not for this that I am calling you. I am doing it to remind you of your internal work."

Tangen goes back to bed thinking that he has gotten out of bed in vain, that his master didn't need him. What does he want? He wants his master to count on him. He projects his father onto his master. His master has become the ideal father to whom he goes as soon as the latter needs him.

Tangen makes a mistake. Learning doesn't mean finding the ideal father under whose shadow you can pretend to look for yourself. It consists of finding yourself. A master helps his disciples find themselves.

That is why, when Tangen starts falling asleep, Echu says

to him, "Oh, attendant, enter into yourself." He calls him three times, hoping he will finally understand. He thinks, "I'm telling him to listen to himself, to enter into his own depths, to do his work. Until he starts serving himself instead of me, he won't find himself."

After the third time, the aide still doesn't understand. He says, "Master, you have called me three times."

"I haven't called you three times. I have told you to find yourself three times. I thought I didn't know how to guide you, but now I see it's not my fault. You have your ears blocked. You hold on to your most superficial personality. When I call you three times without giving you a reason, you're in crisis. Enter into yourself! Understand yourself. And ask for forgiveness."

Gurdjieff calls this "the call to self." Remembering yourself. Not getting into relationships that aren't meant for you, that have nothing to do with you, that are the fruit of projections that feed themselves on your past.

Constant Inconstancy

"Master, what is constant?"
"That which is inconstant."
"How can the inconstant be constant?"
"It's life! It's life!"

The disciple is completely in the intellect. He asks, "What is constant?"

The master answers, "That which is inconstant is constant." Everything changes, and since everything changes, change is the only thing that remains.

It's a good answer, but the disciple adds, "Why is the inconstant constant? Why does change go on?"

His question is still intellectual. The master responds, "It's life! It's life!"

"What is it that neither begins nor ends? Life, and life can't be defined. You won't find anything when you look for it with words."

The Thousand Hands of the Buddha of Compassion

Muyoku approached his master Rinzai and said to him, "Avalokiteshvara, the Bodhisattva of compassion, has a thousand hands and there is an eye on each of them. Which one is the real eye?"

Without even giving him time to breathe, Rinzai immediately examined his disciple's question: "The Bodhisattva of compassion has a thousand hands and there is an eye on each of them. Which is the real one? Answer quickly!"

Muyoku threw Rinzai out of his seat and took his place. Standing, Rinzai said to Muyoku, "Why?" He then made a great roaring sound from his hara *(soft belly) and expelled his disciple from his place. He sat down again. Muyoku said goodbye and left.*

Let us examine this koan. A master is seated. Well seated. Calm reigns in him. A monk enters with his question. He asks, "The Bodhisattva of compassion has a thousand hands and there is an eye on each of them. Which is the real eye?"

Instead of answering, the master quickly returns the question to him in the same terms.

Let's suppose I am Rinzai. I am here, calm, happy, confident. I do not question myself. I am who I am.

I am not like those people who come to ask me, "I'm dating this guy. Is he the man of my life?"

"And you ask me this question? If you have doubts, it means you don't love him."

"Am I a poet?"

"Why do you want an answer? Write! Do it! Don't doubt."

Rinzai has no doubts. He is one with the world. Muyoku comes in with a thousand thoughts in his mind: "What about Buddhism . . . what about this and that . . . and the Buddha of compassion. What is compassion? He has a thousand hands and an eye on each of them . . . they are all false . . . at least one or two of them must be real . . . where are they?"

He comes in with his head full of things. His mind is filled with static, like a radio. The master, hearing his mental confusion, takes up his question and throws it back at him.

Repeating Muyoku's question, Rinzai seizes it from his mouth. Like changing a baby's diaper, the master wipes clean his disciple's mind. He extracts his question as he would excise a tumor.

The master adds, "Answer quickly!" In other words, "When I take the question from your mouth, I rip out your intellect. Respond to me in that state."

Rinzai has performed, thus, an entire psychical operation. The disciple doesn't get it. His static has ceased. He responds, "Since you don't answer and on top of that you steal my question, I'll take your seat."

Rinzai asks, "Why?" In other words, "It's not about taking someone else's place, because if you do so, you enter a competition that has nothing to do with reality. Why do you want my seat? Take yours, take the one that corresponds to you. When you sit in mine, you're not being yourself. What game are you playing?"

He then shouts loudly and recovers his seat, as if saying,

"Everyone has (and should be at) his own place, the one that corresponds to him, where he is himself."

Muyoku makes a respectful gesture toward Master Rinzai and thanks him. He has understood that we're all the Buddha of compassion. That Buddha has a thousand hands—our hands—and a thousand eyes—our consciousness. Which one is real? Yours? Mine? They're all real. When we all live our true nature, no eye is false. At that moment, compassion appears. We all make up a Buddha of a thousand hands and a thousand eyes. We can coexist without competition and act together.

What is compassion? Is it posing intellectual questions like those of the disciple? Is it believing there is only one real thing, when each one of us is real at every moment? Are we going to interpret reality as though we were the only ones to possess it? Christ can say, "I am the way, the truth, and the life," but we cannot. Each one of us is one of those hands, an eye of that whole body that is universal compassion.

When Rinzai says, "Respond quickly," he means, "Eliminate from your spirit those questions that set you apart from the world. Be one with me."

The disciple Muyoku answers by taking Rinzai's seat. The latter says, "What makes you think you will find self-realization by competing? When you take my place, does your consciousness become more real and mine less real? We are both in consciousness, here and now. Wherever you are, consciousness is, and wherever I am, there she is as well. She is in each one of us."

He then shouts. Life is expressed. Muyoku bids Rinzai farewell and leaves. He thanks the master. He has understood the lesson.

The Master's Heart

A bonzo asked his master,
"Are you in your heart?"
The master answered,
"No, I'm not in my heart."

Posing such a stupid question to a master indicates that the bonzo doubts him. Only a disciple can ask such a question. A master can tell with a simple glance whether his inquisitor is in his heart. It is visible. When a person reaches a certain level of consciousness, he sees this level in everyone.

The legend goes that when Buddha reached the state of enlightenment he immediately said, "I have just realized that everybody carries an internal Buddha. He exists inside everyone." These were his first words.

We see our level of consciousness in everyone. Everyone possesses it. On the other hand, everyone possesses every level. It could be said that every human being is a perfection of the universe that gets ignored. Consciousness does not add anything to the self, other than the possibility of seeing its own self at its own level. And the more conscious you are, the more you see yourself. Therefore, a master can perfectly tell whether or not we are in our hearts.

The disciple asks, "Are you in your heart?" And the master responds, "No, I am not in my heart." By this answer he means, "I am not in the heart you imagine, the one you see. What heart do you mean? You speak only about the echelon you know, your level. What does 'your heart' represent to you? I am not in this heart you reference. I am in mine."

The master has thus erased the disciple's projection. He has not sought to exist in someone else's desire or hope. He is not in this world to respond to someone else's expectations.

In a book of Gestalt therapy, psychiatrist Fritz Perls wrote a poem that read more or less like this:

> *I am not in the world to meet your*
> * expectations,*
> *And you are not in the world to meet*
> * mine.*
> *If by chance we find each other, it's*
> * beautiful.*
> *If not, it can't be helped.*

The master tells his disciple, "I am not in the world to meet your expectations. I am in my heart."

Ten Thousand

*One day Master Ummon said to his disciples, "If you don't see
a man for three days, and when he returns you are not sure he
is the same man, what happens to you then?"*

    Nobody answered.

    The master said, "Ten thousand," and departed.

This koan is about continual change. After three days, we are
different. We are never identical to our own selves.

    When the master says, "Ten thousand," it means, "I accept
the ten thousand facets of my inner diamond. Every human
being within me is one of the multiple facets of this diamond.
A personality stuck in repetition does not allow for renewal.
Novelty appears when I see myself as I am in pure consciousness. I accept constant change. I don't restrict myself to limited models of myself. I have the possibility of changing."

    French Impressionist artist Paul Gauguin would never
have become Gauguin if he had not followed this principle.
He was a bank employee for a good part of his life, until the
day he decided he was an artist. That day he left the bank and
became a genius painter.

Stronger than Buddha

"Is there anything that surpasses Buddha, anything that surpasses the patriarch?" the disciple asked Master Ummon.
"Yes," replied the master, "a biscuit."

I love this answer because it's absolutely true. It means that the pleasure of the real surpasses, for sure, any intellectual pleasure. This disciple, like all others, is on an intellectual "trip."

"What's your philosophy?"
"When I eat, I eat. When I dream, I dream."

This is a typical answer. It indicates that I should be where I am. We're trapped inside multiple psychological shells, and the key to escaping those shells is, "What do I feel?" Or "How do I feel deep inside?" It's a very simple key.

"Intellectually, all words aside, how do I feel, here and now, in my intellect? Emotionally, how do I feel, here and now? How do I feel as a being?"

Interior and Exterior

*Manjusri, the Bodhisattva of wisdom, was in the outer part of
a temple.*

*Buddha summoned him from within, saying, "Hey,
Manjusri, why don't you come inside?"*

*Manjusri replied, "Why come inside? I am not under the
impression that I am outside."*

The Best Piece of Meat

*One day while he was wandering at a market, Banzan the
monk heard a client asking for the best piece of meat at the
butcher's shop.*

*"At my shop," the butcher replied, "every piece of meat is
the best. You won't be able to find one that isn't."*

The butcher's answer enlightened Banzan.

Let us say that Buddha symbolizes my internal perfection.
In this case, my wisdom—which is part of this perfection—
cannot be outside of me. Wherever it might be, it will be
inside me. When someone loves, the exterior and the interior
cease to exist. Everything is the center. Everything is united.
My hand is not outside my body.

Manjusri responds, "Why should I come in if I don't feel
like I'm outside? The temple's door is an illusory barrier. It is
symbolic. I am always with you. For me, there is no interior
and exterior."

"Oh, Buenos Aires, I have traveled around the world, but I've never been separated from you," said Argentine poet Jorge Luis Borges. And Saint Thomas said, "A friendship that can end has never been a true friendship."

In the second koan, Banzan is enlightened because he understands that nothing is better than anything else. Every part of us, from our sexuality to our emotional life, our intellect, and our material center, is the best of us. Nothing in us can be considered less good.

To reach the state of enlightenment a human being needs to acknowledge that everything inside him is the best.

In the same way as the universe, we have a dark side and a bright side. The dark side, however, is not our bad side. As Gurdjieff used to say, "A cane always has two ends." Likewise, the two sides of a coin are inextricably linked.

Our dark root is populated by a multiplicity of "things," such as incest, shifting archetypes, homosexual fantasies, jealousy, possessive desires, cannibalism, sadomasochism, and so on. From the moment we recognize this root in ourselves and work on it, it moves forward, evolves, and produces a diamond. It produces the best of us—our consciousness.

It's not a question of the "awareness of something," but our individual light. If we accept it, we live at the best level of ourselves.

Our culture teaches us to remain in a relatively mediocre state of ourselves. It pushes us to live in nothingness, the nothingness that fills us. I know people who feel ashamed of having higher feelings.

It must be said that by all social standards, beauty is forbidden. It is, of course, permissible to shine in industrial, cultural, and educational domains, among others, but this kind of beauty is external to the temple. We give it too much importance, while we are ashamed of affirming our primary beauty—that incomparable beauty that represents the best of us.

Some of our thoughts are true wonders. There is no need to imitate other people's beauty when it is enough to accept our own. This is what I told a graphic artist who showed me his book. I asked him, "Of what use are all those technical skills if you're not yourself? You're nowhere in your drawings. It seems you're more interested in pleasing others than in pleasing yourself. Seek the beauty of your own self. Draw what you really like. Be yourself! Don't get lost trying to show that you have technical ability and run the risk of not being yourself."

People don't dare or can't express their best thoughts. My optimism has often caused a reaction. People say, "Look where the world is headed! How can you think the way you do?"

I understand your reticence, but I want you to notice that I am part of the world. If the world were completely imperfect, it would be perfect. We would all be dark beings and no one would complain or suffer from it. It is the little aspects of perfection, the brief moments of lucidity, that allow us to see the imperfection. We have to develop these. They belong in the world. That's why we have to cultivate the beautiful thoughts that occur in us.

We're better off not resembling one of Dostoyevsky's female characters who allows herself to fall into the abyss for having made a mistake. It's as if we tell ourselves, "I'm worth nothing because my thoughts are ugly." We can say instead, "Maybe I have ugly thoughts, but I also have marvelous dreams.

Sometimes incredible desires and extraordinary thoughts cross my mind. I don't allow myself to express them since I was forbidden from doing so in my childhood. But that doesn't mean these thoughts and desires have ceased to exist."

Just as there are beautiful thoughts, there are also some I wouldn't call exemplary. That would be a wrong way to define them. They are normal thoughts. The other ones, the mediocre ones, are abnormal thoughts.

Our hearts are full of extraordinary thoughts. They aren't hermetic or evil. Let's take pride in our higher feelings even if, sometimes, we must face our own jealousy, possessive desire, lack of self-confidence, and so forth.

We are defined not by our dark side but by our bright side (the jewel that inhabits us). If a piece of rock conceals a diamond within it, the value of the object is not the rock, but rather the diamond. If we possessed such an object, we would preserve it as something valuable, waiting to work on it and to clear away the rock.

I think that emotional life can be compared to a piece of volcanic rock that conceals a diamond within it. That's why we need to guard it and respect it. We shouldn't look down upon it as an ordinary piece of rock, but rather we should give it the importance that the diamond has.

We know superior thoughts, feelings, and desires, but we also know dark desires. Who hasn't dreamed about sleeping with the boss's spouse? Who hasn't desired a friend's girlfriend or boyfriend? Who hasn't had—unwillingly—disturbing thoughts that originate in dreams? Is there anyone who has never had an erotic dream? Is there anyone who has never, in dreams, had sex with a family member? Who hasn't murdered in a dream? We carry all this within ourselves. In these swamps of desire there is nonetheless a longing for light that allows us to find our natural desire, that desire that is comparable to a diamond.

Once we have identified it, we say, "I want to pursue this particular wish and not the thousands of other dreams that come with it." I met a married woman who wanted to be faithful to her husband. She said to me, "I control my desire in a Draconian way, but if I didn't, I would be a nymphomaniac. All men arouse me."

We should find our primordial desire and not surrender ourselves to just any desire. We will thus create within us a path that will take us to our desire of light.

The same happens with our actions. It's better not to do just anything, since every single action is precious, even the crawling of a worm.

Even the smallest action has repercussions. For example, we are going straight ahead on a road and all of a sudden we deviate from our path by an inch. With time, that little deviation drives us away from our initial route, provoking great changes. That is how fundamental changes occur: because on one occasion, in a matter of a second, we make either a bright or a dark decision.

In the second koan, Banzan becomes enlightened because he realizes there are no parts in him that are better than the others.

Intellect, emotional life, sexual and creative life, material center . . . each of our parts possesses a meaning, just as each part of a cow possesses its own. We can't say that one cow is inferior to another unless our criteria are limited to the resistance of our teeth. The cow is neither firm nor tender, soft nor juicy. Only our cannibal side can express itself in such terms. The cow, in and of itself, possesses only good parts. None of them are bad.

The most minor inch of our time has its importance, just as the most minor portions of ourselves have their meanings.

The Three Worlds

One day, a monk asked Master Ganto, "When the three worlds* harass me, shake me, and bother me, what should I do?"

Ganto said, "When the three worlds harass you, sit down."

"I don't understand."

"Do you see this mountain?" Ganto asked. "Bring it here and then I will give you an answer."

The disciple feels anxious because of his desires, his mind, and what happens in the world, and he tries to escape from all that. He asks his master what he should do. The latter replies, "Sit down." By this he means, "Hold on. Meditate."

The disciple expresses his lack of understanding, and Ganto says, "Bring me this mountain."

It is impossible to move a mountain. In this way Ganto tells his disciple, "You ask for the impossible. Your mind will always be here. So will your emotional life and your desires. The world will always be here. If you try to stop it, you will achieve nothing but getting yourself into a crisis, because you will be chasing the impossible. Such is nature. The only thing you can do is enter into yourself, into your real nature. Allow the manifestations of the three worlds to come and go. Attend this event. In the same way you attend a storm, attend your wrath. Stay here. Stay without taking action. Stop reacting to everything that happens."

---

*In the Zen tradition, the three worlds are the world of desire, the mental world, and the material world.

What Has Become of the Old Masters?

One day Kaku said to his master Tokusan, "I suppose all the old masters who have passed away have gone somewhere. Tell me, Master, what has become of them?"

"I don't have the slightest idea," replied Tokusan.

Disappointed, Kaku bitterly observed, "I was expecting the answer of a galloping horse and I receive that of a turtle."

He went away in contempt. Tokusan, seeing him leave, shrugged his shoulders and lifted his eyes helplessly toward the sky. The next morning, after his bath, Tokusan saw that Kaku had proposed having tea together. He asked him, "Have you resolved the koan you formulated to me yesterday?"

Kaku smiled and replied with a satisfied tone, "Master, today your Zen is much better."

Tokusan shrugged his shoulders again and lifted his eyes helplessly toward the sky.

It is important for a disciple not to doubt his master, because it is he who makes the master. The latter reveals himself according to the disciple's expectations. The more the disciple trusts him, the more he will learn from him.

This notion of the master reminds me of a Buddhist phrase that says, "Every event is an opportunity." Everything that happens to us offers the opportunity to transform and develop ourselves, and to grow. It is up to us to take advantage of that opportunity. Each moment reveals itself as a master from the moment we recognize it as such and decide to learn from it.

The fact that Kaku doubts Tokusan indicates from the beginning that he is an imperfect disciple.

One day someone said to me, "A master always wants his disciple to surpass him." It is a debatable point of view. It rather seems that a master stays away from the comparison game. Further, the disciple can't exceed him, since his self-realization belongs to him alone. The disciple will find his own self-realization.

A true master wishes for a disciple to find his own self-realization without competing. He is an instructor. A false master, on the other hand, wants the disciple to trust him with his life and riches.

Kaku wants to know what the old masters have become after death. He thinks about reincarnation and things of that nature. In fact, he is afraid of dying. It is this fear that makes him think about reincarnation. He would like to be reassured about it. He would like to hear someone tell him, "After your death, you will reach the pantheon of the masters. You will find them all there, and like little angels, your days will then go by merrily. After that you will reincarnate, and you will be better in each reincarnation. In the end, you will be worthy. Then you will be liberated from this world and will have access to eternal nirvana. You will be with the divinity and bathe in the wonders of a completely spiritual world. You will be very light. You won't have a body and no sex. You will be happy."

This is what Kaku would like to hear, but the master doesn't give him a response. It's not a problem for Tokusan. Why should he care what has become of others? He is a living master. If his disciple wants to know more, Tokusan could tell him, "You have the answer in front of you."

He doesn't seek to reassure his disciple. He simply tells

him that he ignores whatever has become of them. When asked what happens after death, another master replies, "I have no idea. I haven't died yet."

This master lives in the present. When his time arrives, he will worry about it; but for now, why get bombarded with useless questions? While he lives, he lives. When he eats, he eats. When he lays dying, he will lay dying, and when he dies, he will die.

Kaku doesn't like Tokusan's answer and lets him know it by saying, "I was expecting you to give me an incredible answer, like a metaphysical aspirin, something reassuring, and instead you tell me you don't know. Unbelievable! You're a doddering old man."

The next day, Kaku is still there. He is on his toes, since he has insulted Tokusan, but he still brings him his tea as usual. If he had really thought his master was a doddering old man he wouldn't have known how to respond and would have had to leave immediately.

From the moment we realize that a person doesn't correspond entirely to what we expect of him, we have nothing left to do but to break up the relationship. We write a letter to that person saying more or less this:

> *Even though we worked well together, I am bored of doing it because the smell of both your thoughts and your feelings reminds me of sausage and garlic. And since I'm a vegetarian, I have decided to look for a nice leek instead of staying with the sausage.*
>
> SIGNED, ROSE MARIE

However we do it, we break up the relationship.

Sometimes we need to know how to separate from what limits us. Do we break up with that old family past that we drag behind like a ball and chain? Or shall we keep asking for recognition and tenderness from families that have humiliated us, complicated our lives, and denied us?

We never lose the hope of being—finally, one day—seen and recognized. When are we going to give up all of this? When are we going to stop asking for recognition? When are we going to stop engaging in relationships in which we lose ourselves?

The disciple doesn't break up the relationship. He goes away nagging, and the next day he comes back with the tea as if nothing had happened. Deep inside he must feel uncomfortable. And while serving tea, he must watch for any sign that might give an indication of the master's mood. How will the latter react?

Just as he does every morning, the master takes his tea, and in an excellent mood he asks Kaku whether he has resolved the koan from the night before.

He is cheerful. The fact the he was insulted the night before doesn't bother him at all. When Kaku reproached him then for not answering the question, he shrugged his shoulders helplessly, thinking, "Oh, yes, I haven't responded. You insult me . . . well then, go on with your attitude. I couldn't care less." He is not affected by his disciple's mood.

Kaku, noticing that Tokusan is not upset and that he is even in an excellent mood, feels reassured. He expresses his relief, saying, "Your Zen is much better today."

Since his master has received him well, Kaku feels better. He feels affection for Tokusan once again.

Tokusan, witnessing his disciple's change of mood regarding him, shrugs his shoulders in a sign of hopelessness. It is his way of saying, "Look, my friend, I couldn't care less about your outbursts of rage and your praise. I am what I am. Your mood isn't going to change my internal truth that I realize the Buddha within me. I do not live my life waiting to see what you think about me. Your thoughts are not going to elevate me or degrade me, because I am myself and in no way do I depend on what you think or believe. And also, I feel quite well today. The tea is excellent."

We make so many projections! We want others to become our father or mother. We create expectations. And when the expectations we have built are shattered, when they reveal themselves differently from what we expected, we feel disappointed, betrayed, and even desperate. That is because we are the ones who venerate idols and we are the ones who break them down. We spend our lives knocking idols off the pedestals we've created for them.

The interesting thing about this koan lies in its emphasis on the importance of living and acting in accordance with one's own heart, rather than trying to meet someone else's expectations.

A Definition of Zen

Te-Chan, who was Chuei-ien's best disciple, went to see his master one day and said to him, "Master, I have learned a lot from you, but now it seems imperative for me to travel around China to perfect my knowledge of Buddhism."

With Chuei-ien's blessing, Te-Chan left the monastery. He traveled for many years throughout China and one day he went back to see Chuei-ien. The latter received him and said, "So you have traveled around China."

"Yes, Master."

"Summarize Zen Buddhism in a few words."

Te-Chan concentrated, and after reflecting for a moment, he said, "When clouds stop above the mountain peak, moonlight cannot penetrate the water of the lake."

"Oh," said the master, "your hair has turned gray and you've lost some teeth. Is that all you have managed to learn about Zen? What a disappointment!"

Te-Chan burst into tears. He then asked Chuei-ien, "And you, Master, give me your summary of Zen."

"Well, I'll tell you my summary. When clouds stop above the mountain peak, moonlight cannot penetrate the water of the lake."

Transformed by this answer, the disciple said, "Thank you, Master! I have become enlightened."

In the same way, the master of this koan could ask his disciple:

"What is solitude?"

The disciple could answer what solitude is not and say,

"Solitude is not knowing how to be with yourself."

"Idiot! Your answer is incorrect!"

"What is solitude then, Master?"

"Solitude, my friend, is not knowing how to be with yourself."

"Thank you, Master! You have just taught me a great truth."

This koan is truly enigmatic. It reminds me of another one.

Two monks were meditating, each in a different cabin. The master went to visit them. He opened the door of the first cabin and asked the disciple how he was. He answered by lifting a lit match in front of his face. The master slapped him and the monk had to apologize many times.

The master then went to see the second disciple. He asked him the same question and the latter gave him the same answer: he lifted a lit match in front of his face.

Fascinated, the master congratulated him.

I didn't understand why the master had such different reactions to the same answer. There was something about it that seemed illogical to me.

Let us reexamine the first koan. When we decide to work with a master, we should trust him wholeheartedly and not leave him until the moment we ourselves have become masters. If we leave before that, we will not have completed the work. In this case we would be wandering from one master to the other without covering more than "a mile." We would go from question to question and receive only answers.

When we pose a question, we receive a verbal answer. But what is the value of these kinds of answers? How is it beneficial for us to be told these things?

When Te-Chan is near his master, he has the truth within reach. However, he prefers to leave. He tours a great distance looking for the truth and then returns to his master thinking he knows quite a bit. He believes it because he can say it all, explain it all.

When his master, Chuei-ien, asks him for a summary of Zen, Te-Chan tells him a deep and serious truth: The mountain—that is, me, I am the mountain—meditates. But clouds come. The clouds symbolize the protective shells I carry with me—intellectual, emotional, and sexual shells. They form a kind of ceiling of false thoughts, false feelings, and false desires that imprison me in my ego and push me away from knowledge.

The moon. In becoming enlightened the monk said, "Oh, bright, bright moon!" He had found ecstasy. Life is ecstasy.

Jung advocated that "free association can lead from any one dream to the critical secret thoughts that torment individuals." These secret thoughts that torment us are the clouds. When we perceive them—in other words, when we perceive our suffering—we fall into the ecstasy that lives within us. To be alive is to live in ecstasy. This is what Te-Chan says.

When the moon—that is, existential happiness—penetrates through the thoughts that torment me, when it penetrates my unconscious, the waters of the lake—my life—then I become a "bright, bright moon." There is no difference between the moon and me. I have no need to reflect it. I am it. I am outside time and space. I am inside reality itself.

This is what Te-Chan tells his master regarding Zen. But the latter isn't fooled by this answer. He says, "You are telling me what Zen is. You think about it. You maybe even teach others, but you haven't made it a reality."

When he then defines Zen using exactly the same words as his disciple, it is the moon that speaks. It expresses an experience he knows and lives all the time.

A truth expressed by someone who has made it reality is not the same as the same truth expressed by someone who possesses only an intellectual knowledge of it.

When we haven't done something, we can only talk about it. When we have done it, we don't talk about it, we live it.

We can then speak about it using the same symbols everyone else uses (the mountain, the clouds, the penetrating moon). The difference is that we are profoundly present in our definition and it becomes true because it is lived.

Facing Disaster

A disciple said to Joshu, "Master, when facing disaster, what do you do to avoid it?"

Joshu opened his arms, took a deep breath, and said with a big smile, "This is what is."

The disciple says: "When a disaster occurs, how can we avoid it?"

"Disasters don't exist."

The term itself qualifies it—the awareness of the disaster is what creates the disaster.

Ultimately, when we are in a seemingly catastrophic situation, we should realize that what happens to us isn't horrible. We could say, as Joshu did, "This is what is." Everything that happens to us is amazing. We are in the middle of the "thing" and it is "what is." We cannot call it disaster. We should call it life with its contradictions, its crises, and its multiple facets. In the midst of what is called disaster, we are in "what is." If someone sues me in court, "That is what is." If my relationship is in crisis, "This is what is."

With such a state of mind, we do not avoid life and its mishaps. On the contrary, we situate ourselves in the middle of the catastrophe. We face the event, we say, "This is what is," and we live. At that moment, the disaster ceases to exist. Only life is left, with all that is avoidable and unavoidable. All mixed up.

When Joshu responds, "This is what is," accepting the event, delighted, he is not giving intellectual advice. He shows us he is present. He also shows that if we need to talk about disaster, there is only one—the disciple and his intellectual questions.

When people complain about their situations, I am tempted to tell them, "This is what is," but they are too absorbed in their suffering or problems to accept it. They don't understand that we can tell ourselves, "Listen, what is happening to you is not a catastrophe. Don't try to avoid it. Live!"

My father just got married a second time. His new wife is throwing him a birthday party and hasn't invited my siblings or me. That's outrageous. I asked my siblings whether or not we should just show up. Don't you realize what's happening? She is preventing us from going to our father's birthday party.

Your father has a new wife. "That's what is." If they invite you, "that's what is." If they don't invite you, "that's what is." Why do you think of this event as a disaster? Why do you see it in a negative light?

My son never telephones me. I am desperate.

If your son wants to call you, he calls you. "That's what is." If he doesn't want to call you, he doesn't. "That's also what is."

It's difficult to talk to people about detachment because, in general, they are very attached to things and cannot liberate themselves.

A mystic is precisely someone who knows how to liberate himself from his ties, in the same way that a ship anchors itself in port but, at the moment of setting sail, releases the ropes that secured it to the dock.

Tchao-Tcheu Tests an Old Woman

A monk at Tchao-Tcheu's monastery asked an old woman, "What is the way to Mount Tai?"*

"Straight ahead," she said.

When the monk took a couple of steps forward, she added, "It's foolish to go this way."†

The monk told Tchao-Tcheu the story. The latter said, "Hold on! I will test that old woman on your behalf."

The next day he encountered her and asked her the same question. The old woman gave him the same answer. On returning to the monastery, Tchao-Tcheu told the monks, "I have tested the old woman of Mount Tai on your behalf."

Although it is not clearly explained here, the old woman was a nun. At that time there were enlightened nuns who tested the monks.

She offered the same answer to both master and disciple. That is, she advised Tchao-Tcheu to go straight ahead, and then, when the monk had taken a couple of steps forward, she said, "It's foolish to go this way."

The koan ends at this point. It doesn't seem logical and it seems even useless. Completely useless. What is the point of such a story? What interest can it have for our daily lives? The commentaries that come with it are not necessarily more comprehensible.

---

*Mount Tai is the location of a temple reputed to dispense valuable spiritual teachings.

†In another translation, she says, "You are an ordinary monk like all the others."

The Mocking Gloss of Wu-Men

The old woman knows the agenda, but she doesn't recognize the spy following her. Old Tchao-Tcheu inserts himself in the enemy camp, threatens the stronghold, but does not deserve the title of Great Man. In the end, I find them both in the wrong. So tell me, why does Tchao-Tcheu test the old woman?

Wu-Men adds to his commentary a four-verse poem:

> *The question was the same*
> *and so was the answer.*
> *When there is sand in the cooked rice,*
> *there are thorns in the clay.*

What would a master who has an ashram think about one of his disciples asking a nun, who seems enlightened, the way to a temple where people seek enlightenment? He would say the disciple is a fool and he might even ask, "What is this guy doing with me if he's asking an old woman the way?"

To begin with, it would be interesting for him to know the way on his own. But no, he doesn't.

We have to be loyal to the teachings we receive at a given place, and more so when there aren't really any teachings to be received. We know these teachings consist of awakening our own qualities. We are going to be taught what we are.

For that, there is no need to go learn something here and there. We trust someone, and since we have chosen him as a master, it is for life, so long as he doesn't disappoint us.

Tchao-Tcheu was a master. Why was this monk asking

an old woman questions and looking for a mountain with a mythical temple to connect with the sacred? Why didn't he look for the sacred within himself, since the sacred is inside us?

Gurdjieff used to say that God, noticing that men were so destructive, decided to hide the truth within men's hearts in order to protect it. And it remained thus guarded, since men don't care about their hearts.

This story is beautiful, but in a negative sense. I think we ourselves are the temple and the monastery.

First, why ask an enlightened old woman the way to Mount Tai? And second, why humiliate yourself by telling others about your defeat? Because the disciple has been totally humiliated. He goes to his master to complain. He tells him with a plaintive tone, "Oh, Master, that nun tortured me. I asked her humbly, very humbly, where the temple was. She said, 'Straight ahead,' so I believed her and I went straight ahead because I wanted to go to the temple. And then, Master, she assumed a different position and mocked me for going straight ahead as she'd advised.

"I wasn't asking her how to get to my inner God or my consciousness. I wasn't asking for myself. I wanted to go to the temple! She mocked me because she said, 'Straight ahead,' meaning that to reach the state of enlightenment, we need to go straight ahead to ourselves. We need to shoot arrows to our own hearts.

"She mocked me in that way. She is peculiar, Master. I admire her somewhat because she taught me a harsh lesson. To look for your own spirit you need to go straight to yourself, but you certainly don't have to climb a mountain."

If you ask me, "How can I become enlightened?" I will

tell you, "Meditate. Go straight to yourselves. Enter your own treasure." If you thank me and go straight ahead to Mount Tai, I will treat you as a stubborn man for coming here to ask the way.

Think deeply! There is no other way to find yourself. There is none. Some people can be helpful, of course.

A monk from Tchao-Tcheu's monastery asked an
old woman . . .

She is a woman. Buddhists are very anti-feminist. They would like a woman to reincarnate as a man to become enlightened. They also say that in order to meditate in the lotus position, women should put a heel in front of their sex lest a serpent might penetrate it. I can't imagine what image they have of women's sex.

They have always mistrusted women. Buddha abandoned his woman. Tchao-Tcheu didn't have one.

It is a nun, an enlightened nun, who humiliates the monk. He arrives humiliated at the school.

It is as if I were a karate student in a Hong Kong film. I would come in from the direction of the *dojo*. I would find an old woman and ask, "How can I get to the dojo where they teach martial arts?" and the old lady would punch me in the nose. I would arrive humiliated and bleeding in the presence of the master and I would say, "She has broken my nose, Master. What are your teachings worth if I cannot figure out what the old woman told me? I have understood nothing. What is the value of your teachings?"

What does the master respond? Completely absorbed

in himself, he says, "I will test her. Let's see what happens." Cocksure, he sets out to encounter the old woman and brazenly asks her, "Excuse me, Madam, what way should I take to get to Mount Tai?"

"Straight ahead." As he continues in the direction indicated, she adds, "Idiotic old man!"

He comes back to the monastery and proudly announces to his disciples, "My friends, I have tested the old lady."

What should we make of this? We could read it this way. It might be a caricature of a reading, but I don't think so. A master cannot be like this.

The first thing we think is that he is going to test her, but if the master goes to see the old woman it is to teach his disciples a lesson. It is not to teach the old woman a lesson, nor to defeat her. A disciple is a disciple! He must follow teachings in a school for monks, and when he becomes enlightened he will become a master. A disciple is a disciple and a master is a master.

The master thus approaches the old woman. He approaches her as a master, but according to tradition and to my own opinion, he is dressed like a monk, not like a master. He dresses like a disciple, since he introduces himself as a disciple. That is to say, he goes to meet her in disguise, without revealing anything about himself.

He arrives in the presence of the old woman, who, in fact, is visibly a master, since she is seated there to annoy the monks and test them. He comes to her as a monk, and as a monk he asks her, "What is the way to Mount Tai?" He doesn't ask it for himself, since he knows it already. Nor does he ask for spiritual knowledge. He asks only a practical question, "How does one get to Mount Tai?"

She doesn't recognize him. She treats him like a disciple. She says, "Straight ahead." She gives him an automatic answer. She gives him the same advice.

A master enlightened people by showing them his raised thumb. A disciple made the same gesture and the master asked him, "Show me what you do to make people enlightened."

"I do the same thing you do, Master, the same gesture," he responded, raising his thumb.

The master cut off his thumb with a swipe of his sword, and then the disciple understood.

I don't know what he understood, but he understood. Now instead of lifting his thumb, he lifts his pinky.

Tchao-Tcheu thus comes before the old woman and she doesn't recognize the master in him. She treats him like a disciple and says, "Straight ahead." He goes straight ahead and she adds, scornfully, "You are like all the rest!" The master continues walking. He has tested the old woman.

Why did he test her? To show that this woman cannot recognize a master. When she tests the monks, she does it purely to assert herself. She can't tell one disciple from another. She sees only the appearance but not the level of qualification. She doesn't need to teach everybody a spiritual lesson. Sometimes people simply need to know the correct direction. Not everything is symbolic.

He didn't tell this to the old woman. She can, therefore, continue to lie, gesticulate, and play her role; he doesn't give a damn. He cares about his disciples.

When he comes back, he tells them, "She has been tested."

The disciples ask, "What did you say to her?"

"I asked her how to get to Mount Tai."

"What did she answer?"

"Straight ahead."

"And what did you do?"

"I went straight ahead."

"And what did she say?"

"She said I was an idiot. I tested her."

"Thank you, Master."

Since they know their master, they realize the woman's error and undoubtedly say to themselves, "How dare this woman say to you the same thing she says to us? She is blind! She is deaf! She doesn't understand anything!"

It is a very anti-feminist story. With this we are done judging the woman. Now let us judge the master by reading again the commentary.

This is the mocking gloss:

The old lady knows her agenda , , ,

She knows how to ask precise questions. With this question, "Where are you going?" and then "Straight ahead," she has a good agenda.

But she doesn't see the spy who follows her.

That is to say, she doesn't realize that the master is coming not to meet her as a victim (since she has an agenda), but rather to see her just as she is. She can design an agenda, but she cannot live up to her plan.

> *The old Tchao-Tcheu inserts himself in the*
> *enemy's camp . . .*

He enters in disguise. The spy is disguised as a monk and looks just like his disciple.

> *But although he threatens the stronghold, he*
> *doesn't deserve the title of Great Man.*

Let's see why he doesn't deserve it.

> *It the end, both explanations seem wrong*
> *to me. Tell me, then, why Tchao-Tcheu*
> *tests the old woman.*

Why does he need to test her? To teach his disciples something, whatever it is, or to show the old woman that she's not worth much? And why does he need to prove this to himself or to others? What need does he have to mount a campaign, become a spy, compete, enter into combat? What need does he have to do all this? None. What this means is that he is expressing his acrimony toward nuns, and that's it! That's what he has expressed. He has argued with someone who wasn't of his rank. He has tested her. But to what effect? None. That is why he is mistaken. On the spiritual path we shouldn't be showing off our values.

The master has no need to compare himself to anyone or show anyone what he knows. Even if he can discredit the other person, he doesn't need to do it to be worth something. Why? A light illuminates an entire city. Zen tradition says,

"When a flower blossoms, it is spring all around the world." When you do something truly positive, it can change the world. The things that have changed the world have been true and powerful things in their time. It is not negativity that has done it. Those things have wrought destruction.

When somebody starts thinking correctly, he is like a well-tuned harpsichord. He sounds as he should. He doesn't need to demonstrate anything. The master doesn't need to demonstrate anything. He doesn't need to do anything and that is enough.

It is then that we can understand the poem. It becomes clear, like the water of a spring.

The question was the same,
as was the answer.

The question was the same. But who asks the question? It's not the question itself that matters. What matters is who asks it. When a fool tells you, "It doesn't start, it doesn't end, what is it?" it's foolishness. But it's a different question when someone who has achieved the highest spiritual rank asks, "It doesn't start, it doesn't end, what is it?" In other words, the question will change depending on the spiritual level of the person formulating it.

The answer was the same. If someone responds in the same way to the same question being asked by different people, that person is not perceptive. It's similar to the story of the master I mentioned before, the one who visits the monks in their chambers.

The master opens the door of the first one and the monk

lifts a lamp before the master's face. The master says, "Well done." The master then opens the second chamber, the monk lifts a lamp before the master's face, and the master slaps his face.

Both monks have done exactly the same thing, but the master sees the difference. The same answer given by two people is different. Words pronounced by people at different spirituals levels are different.

The old woman always answers in the same way. What should we think about a person who cannot see the spiritual level of her questioner? It's as if a judo expert were unable to distinguish between a white belt and a black belt; his life would be in danger. He would need to be able to recognize the difference. In the realm of the spiritual there are also different degrees.

People think that because they think and exist they are already in possession of the truth and can evaluate everything, but it's not so. There are levels. There is work to be done and some people have done their job and others haven't. With time, those who haven't done their jobs pay the price. Yes, they pay.

And here are two mysterious phrases:

When there is sand in the cooked rice,
there are thorns in the clay.

When there is sand in the cooked rice. There is sand in the old woman's rice. This means she has flaws—she functions mechanically. Her enlightenment is imperfect.

There are thorns in the clay. The master has thorns. In other words, there is something aggressive in him.

From the moment we decide to compare ourselves to someone who has sand in the rice, we have thorns in the clay. If the master hadn't had thorns in the clay, he would not have tested the old woman. He would have done his job, remaining at ease with his internal peace. He would have nothing to prove. Nothing to demonstrate. Spiritual work is a work we do within ourselves in profound peace.

There is nothing to teach. We can guide, not teach. There is nothing to transmit. All that nonsense about the transmission of the lamp . . . Nothing is transmitted. The lamp has already been transmitted.

You want me to give you my lamp? You're a fool. You want me to blow up yours? I can't. Blow up your own lamp! As you do it, I will transmit the lamp to you. (I speak on behalf of Tchao-Tcheu.)

What lamp have I transmitted to you? "For to everyone who has, more will be given, and from the one who has not, even the little he has will be taken away from him." Do you remember this phrase from the Gospel? Or this phrase from Zen: "If you have a cure, I'll give you a cure. If you don't, I'll take it from you."

It's always the same. If you have, I'll give you, I'll transmit the lamp to you, but if you don't do your job, I'll take it away. In other words, I give you nothing. I don't care at all. I am not going to mix myself with your rice full of sand.

That is the transmission of the lamp. Don't be deluded. There is nothing to be handed to you. No treasure to be given to you. No direction to be given, such as "The mountain is this way. Go straight ahead."

For me, going straight ahead means following a twisting

path like the labyrinth at Chartres Cathedral, since I'm pretty complex. Why should I go straight ahead the way everybody else does? I have the right to move forward as I wish, as long as I move forward, as long as I feel well, and as long as I achieve my evolutionary development.

If we do a psychological interpretation of this koan, we have to ask why the nun is spiteful. She is spiteful because the monk is so as well. It's mom and dad. The nun chastises the children because she cannot see the man in her husband, in her master. She sees a child. She denies his masculinity. From her point of view, he is not an adult. She lectures him. In short, she thinks of herself as the universal mother who is always teaching lessons.

Many women who have not had a father fall into this foolishness, which also happens to many men who have had no mother. These women, like the nun, have this flaw because, not having had a father, they haven't been able to internalize their masculine side. However, they carry the master in themselves, because we all have a masculine side and a feminine side. We are men and women, yin and yang.

This woman needs, therefore, to reduce all men to the level of children. In this way, the man will never exist. A woman like this will always be a universal mother, the great goddess surrounded by little children.

The opposite happens with men who haven't recognized their mothers. They become grandfathers surrounded by children.

The nun ignores what puts sand in the rice and the master ignores what puts thorns in the clay. Had they both recognized each other in their level of spiritual development, they would not have interfered with the monk; they would not have interfered with the children.

If parents recognized each other, they would let their children grow up in peace. And even if they didn't live together, they would come up with ways to distance the children from battles that concern only adults—self-proclaimed adults who are nothing but children.

Do you understand the way I use this koan? It is a mutual lack of recognition that provokes this lack of enlightenment. A time comes when we need to recognize ourselves.

Since working with this koan, I have asked myself what a master is. How does a master feel?

Let's suppose that the master (not Tchao-Tcheu, who bungled the situation) has recognized himself. He's realized that he shouldn't continue fighting with his father or his mother. That's not it! He has to stop fighting with the parental archetypes within himself. That is, he must accept his humanity.

Once we have accepted the mother and the father as universal principles, despite how much we have suffered (the majority of us have suffered in childhood, irrespective of our parents, perhaps due to society, a historical moment, or something else), then we can manage to release ourselves from this shell, from this superego, by absorbing it. When it is absorbed, we stop competing and stop disparaging. We have a kind of learned modesty that consists of not accepting our value.

A master is someone who humbly accepts his value. Who will decide what that value is and isn't? He himself.

He will say, "How do I feel? Who am I?" First he will answer, "I am who I am," as in the Bible. It's excellent to be able to say, "I am who I am."

At that point, the performance has ended. In the intellect, I am who I am with whatever power I may have. In the emotional sense, I am who I am. In the sexual sense, in my entire self, "I am who I am."

Is it enough? No. We should add, "I was who I was. I will be who I will be. I am who I was and I am who I will be."

Here is the master. He unconditionally accepts his past, present, and future. In this moment he is everything he has been in his lives and in eternal lives, and everything he will be in his lives and in eternal lives until the moment he reaches the sensation of being all one. It will feel global.

Human beings arrive at similar states—feeling the oneness. At the same time, they can feel inconsequential.

The master feels inconsequential. He feels life passes in the snap of a finger. Why worry whether we will die tomorrow or a hundred years from now, when in the end we will still die? It is useless to worry about it, because even if it's a long time away, it's short—the snap of a finger.

Since he can act in the meantime, the master focuses on each passing moment. He can even prolong his life a little by opening up to the intensity of its vital moments.

He opens up to mental intensity. Not insanity, but the expanding mind. He opens to the intensity of the emotional, the intensity of creativity (be it sexual, be it artistic), and to the intensity of the substance of his life. It is intense, very intense. It has nuisances, it grows old, but it is intense. He lives in the intensity of a universal force.

This is how Master Tchao-Tcheu should have been and how Wu-Men must have been.

Arakuine's Tears

The monk Arakuine was weeping. His friend asked him, "Why are you crying?"

Arakuine answered, "Go ask the master."

He went and asked the master, "Why is Arakuine crying?"

"Go ask him!" replied the master.

The monk went back to join Arakuine and found him laughing. He said, "How can it be? You were crying before, and now you're laughing. Why?"

Arakuine answered, "Because I was crying before and now I am laughing."

If I feel like crying, I cry. Why repress myself? The sky is blue, a storm comes, rain comes. But then the rain goes away. And when he asks me, "Why are you crying?" I say, "Go ask the master—your master, go ask yourself. You enter into yourself and you see yourself crying. When you cry, cry. When you eat, eat. When you get angry, get angry. Don't repress your wrath! Set yourself loose. Ask yourself. Be a transparent blue sky. And when you feel like crying, cry, and then, if you feel like laughing, laugh. The storm has passed and the birds are singing. Let things come and go with an immense pleasure."

What a pleasure it is to burst into anger! It's a discharge of energy. It's wonderful. And depression? It's wonderful. In fact, we know that this is not what we are. And pain? And illness? It's all wonderful! This is not what we are, not at all.

We are the blue sky, and we don't identify with these states of being. It's enough! Afterward we can let in the light. In the light, there are shadows and other things, but it is always light. No effort. No mental effort. Nothing. Calm. We don't need to make an impression.

Enlightenment

A master tells his disciple, "No one has ever achieved enlightenment," and the disciple becomes instantly enlightened.

No one has ever achieved enlightenment, simply because we are all enlightened. Enlightenment is not something to be achieved; everything is enlightened. We work and work to achieve it, but it's not achievable, one *is* enlightened. That is enlightenment. All human beings are enlightened. The whole world is perfect.

The Candle

A monk spends the day with an old master. At night he is ready to return home, but the night is very dark. He goes to the master and says, "I can't go home because of the darkness."

The master says, "Wait, I'll give you a candle."

He takes a lit candle to hand to the monk, but at the moment he is about to give it to him, he blows it out and the disciple becomes enlightened.

In blowing out the candle the master is saying, "You are the candle. You are the light. Don't come to me asking for light. We are all in darkness. Darkness is light. We are all enlightened. Reality is the same for all of us."

A young man once asked me, "What sound does a tree make when it falls in the forest and no one hears it?"

I answered, "Kaboom!"

It might seem counterintuitive to say "Kaboom!" when no one hears it. But it is not about the tree, it is about ourselves. This means, "Make the phenomenon real. Don't let them come to you with stories. Don't let them do it for you. Listen to yourself. It has no importance whether anyone else listens to you or not. Make the phenomenon real by yourself. To achieve it, accept yourself. Accept once and for all that you don't need your daddy! Daddy blows out the candle and says, 'Go into the darkness and find yourself.'"

The Master's Gratitude

As custom dictates, a disciple arrives in the presence of a great Zen master with a gift. The master receives the gift, and as the only sign of gratitude, he strikes his disciple five times with a cane. The latter, bruised and confused, asks, "Why do you hit me?"

Without saying a word, the master hits him another five times and sends him away. Humiliated, the disciple goes home without having understood anything. He goes to see his own master, explains to him what happened, and asks him why the great master struck him. His master, too, wordlessly strikes him five times with a cane.

The disciple ends up with fifteen bumps on his head, and we ask ourselves why these Japanese people always cane each other. They become predictable in their customs!

I relate this koan to that of the two monks meditating in their chambers who each lift a lamp when the master visits them. Both receive the master the same way, but the master congratulates one and reprimands the other.

The disciple comes in with a gift. The problem is that it happens in a mechanical way. The master then brings him back to self-awareness through pain. He creates a conflict. He hits him five times.

The disciple doesn't understand and asks, "Why?" And the master strikes him with the cane five more times, which means, "Stop running in circles around yourself! Enter into yourself."

The disciple asks for explanations because the master hit him; he tries to engage him. However, that is not the master's business. That is not his concern. The master hits him once more and sends him away, as though saying, "Get out of here! You're incapable of understanding anything."

The disciple then goes to his own master's house and his master says to him, "You want explanation after explanation. Enter into yourself!"

And you, the only way you have to enter into yourself is through pain. You have no other option.

The first monk lifts his lamp before the master. It is a symbol, but it is a deeply felt symbol. The other one does exactly the same but does not have the feeling behind it. He deserves five strokes of the cane.

It's very simple: either we act from our deepest selves or we just scratch the surface. Only someone who looks at you deeply from the exterior can tell whether you have detached yourself from what needs to be let go.

HAIKUS

Please note that the 5-7-5 haiku syllable pattern is in the Japanese version, not the English translation.

Mono izawu
Kyaku to teishu to
Shiragiku to.

Wordless are
the host, the guest,
and the white chrysanthemum.

Truth seekers don't follow one path. In reality, all paths lead to it. But we want to "arrive" somewhere, we want to "have things," while the truth is here. Seeking the truth is precisely a call to "live ourselves."

That's why we seek self-realization through masters, through people we admire and who give us love. There are many ways to "find it," but the poem says, "Truth is here. There's no more truth but what lies within you. Based on this truth, you are yourself and you are the other."

Why doesn't the other appear in my life? Because I don't appear in my own life. And if I don't appear in my own life, how can the other ever do so? If I am a hollow carcass, how can I find the other? Two hollow carcasses approach each other, saying, "Love me, please! Love me." How can anyone love the other if they are both hollow?

The legend says that millions of little Buddhas came together on a mountain peak where the great Buddha was supposed to give a speech. All the monks were waiting, but he didn't say a word. He just showed them a flower. Only one of his disciples smiled, and he was the one to carry on his teachings. This legend is known as "The Sermon of the Flower."

Zen is completely based on people who have that understanding when they are shown a flower.

> *Wordless are*
> *the host, the guest,*
> *and the white chrysanthemum.*

Isn't it beautiful? You came to see me because I am the host and you are the guest. I have prepared a suitable setting for our encounter, so that it may take place without worries, emotional trauma, or painful memories, regardless of our names, our successes, our appetites for power, and our physical anxieties. It's the tea ceremony.

There's a little door you can peek through before entering, to escape from the old image you have of yourself. You bow, you enter, and you meet with me. What do we have to tell each other? We have to stop saying anything at that moment. We are facing each other, you and I, with great pleasure in a relaxed universe, calm, with just your beauty and mine. We have left behind prejudice and self-doubt. We are in absolute beauty. Not the seductive beauty of acquiring something, but the beauty of living creatures, simply because we are alive.

We are together, you and I, and what have I done? I have put on an adornment. An adornment that is a companion. It is that white chrysanthemum that I cut from my garden.

If I cut you off, I suffer. If I don't cut you off, I suffer. Oh, chrysanthemum!

There is a story about a general who likes white chrysanthemums, and a tea master with a white chrysanthemum garden. The great general says, "I will go visit him to see his white chrysanthemums." He leaves the battlefield and goes with all his troops to see the tea master and admire his garden. When he arrives, there are no chrysanthemums. They've been all cut. Enraged, he does not want to bow when he crosses the entry. And what does he see? "In a jar, the most beautiful one is for you." Oh! He understands. It's a marvelous work of poetry. The tea master sacrificed his entire garden for a single white chrysanthemum.

I have sacrificed all the thoughts in my head for one single word called a *mantra*. Of all my parasitic thoughts, I have only one left. I have sacrificed all others in order to keep only love for you, and your acceptance.

Likewise, the white chrysanthemum is silent. It is the one that expands silence. It is white, it is pure, it is unique, it is how it is. Am I, myself, how I am? Are you, yourself, how you are? At this moment, guided by the white chrysanthemum, we begin to abandon the destructive agenda we were given, all the self-criticism and false hopes, the neurotic search for an answer to the eternal question: Who are we?

We are here. We feel ourselves living, relaxed. We enter into our silence, which is not silence. It's life itself that is here.

It's an awareness facing another awareness. We are two mirrors facing each other. We have understood the lesson from the white chrysanthemum and we create a wonderful atmosphere where silence reigns, where the ego, little by little, does not dissolve itself but rather becomes transparent. You and I are transparent, calm. We allow ourselves to take a break from our misfortunes, from our fights. We are here, calm.

We accept each other. Our bodies live their own lives. Time lives its own rhythm. And we enter into an incredible peace—the moment of taking a cup of tea. What matters is not the cup of tea, but being able to reach this state.

This means you are the white chrysanthemum. This means that your body, your *self,* is completely pure, white. It is how it is. We are not used to living in a pure body.

Who has defeated rancor, anxiety, anguish, doubt? Where is the white chrysanthemum? It's difficult, when we feel deeply guilty, to understand the silence of the white chrysanthemum. And all of a sudden:

> *Mono izawu*
> *Kyaku to teishu to*
> *Shiragiku to.*

What does this mean?

They are wordless: *Mono izawu.*

The host—Kyaku; the guest—Teishu; and the white chrysanthemum—*shiragiku.* But silence is there: *Kyaku to! Teishu to! Shiragiku to! Ku to!*

So, if I am the white chrysanthemum, my body reaches the state of *to,* of silence. I am the guest, the ego, and my ego says "to." I am the essential being, the guest, and the essential being says "to." The essential being seeks us. He doesn't leave us alone!

There's a haiku that says, "The cloud allows the monk to stop staring at the moon." Leave me alone, leave me alone! Stop! I'm fed up. You're everywhere. Leave me at least a little corner. But no. Before I was born, you were already here. When I die, you will still be here. You are with me all the time. I can't get even a little bit of distance. It's an ongoing wonder. The activity never stops.

So stop searching for yourself! You no longer fear your intensity, your eternity, your infinity. You cast off your father who tortured you, your mother who ignored you, the society that crushed you, all the people who deceived you, the women who cheated on you, and the men who left you behind with a baby in your arms. You leave all that behind and go back to wonderment. You stop believing you are an empty space that needs to be filled.

Long night
The sound of water
Say what I think.

It's like this. When the poet says, "Long night," we have to think he is full of pleasure, alive, enjoying the adventure of a sleepless night. By himself, alone with the night.

As soon as the sun begins to disappear, I start perceiving the coming of night and the changes that take place within me.

So I then start following the night, living the night, and what does the night talk about? The absolute absence of light. We don't talk about the moon when it appears. We don't talk about the moon but about the night, and somewhere, I am the night. There is a mysterious darkness within me that constantly lives in me since I was born. All my life, since birth, I have always feared this dark side of myself, yet it has always been there.

When you have lived your night once and for all, you no longer have nightmares because nothing in your inner self gets in your way.

I begin to enter the night and the river flows, flows, flows. It doesn't stop. It goes on. The sound of water!

Nagaki yoya
Ommou koto iu
Miso no oto.

Long night
The sound of water
Says what I think.

Beautiful, isn't it? Five syllables, seven syllables, five syllables: ta ta ta ta ta / ta ta ta ta ta ta ta / ta ta ta ta ta.

> Proposition (five syllables): ta ta ta ta ta
> Development (seven syllables): ta ta ta ta ta ta ta
> Resolution (five syllables): ta ta ta ta ta (similar to the proposition)

The answer is included in the proposition. There's nothing to search for, nothing. I live: ta ta ta ta ta. I die: ta ta ta ta ta. Here it is! It's simple, easy, uniform, birth, ever-flowing river, long night that never stops, nothingness that never stops, beauty.

Oh my beloved, my beloved! Enter into my long night . . . the sound of water will tell you what I think. You are the sound of water!

It is the spring wind
Say master and servant
We walk the path together.

When the wind or the Divine Spirit blows, your ego and your essential self are one and the same. The kimonos of the master and the servant blow the same way. Facing the onslaught of the divine wind, what difference is there between my master and me? None. There is no difference. We are equal.

To cut her, what a pity!
To leave her, what a pity!
Oh, this violet!

I must forgo my wish to save my life and my idea not to save it. It's the violet that matters, not my wish to use it. We must live in this world without wishing to use it, being happy with ourselves, just like the violet, the humble violet.

I came back furious
Offended
The willow in the garden.

What does the plant care about my wrath, my emotional catastrophe? She is there. I am stupid for succumbing to these fussy worries, these little neuroses, these outbursts of wrath. On the other hand, if I take some distance and see the onset of my rage and sadness as if they were beautiful plants, then I can experience them in a different way. I can realize that all this is beautiful, that these feelings are here to beautify life and not to make it ugly. Right now, I live my jealousy crisis all alone and say nothing.

The kitten
weighed in the balance
keeps playing.

The kitten remains the same, whether we weigh her or not.
She doesn't care if she's good, bad, fat, or slim. She keeps on
playing! As we say in English, "As long as I'm warm, let them
laugh." Why would I care if people laugh at me if I'm warm
and cozy? I have a ridiculous coat but it keeps me warm,
so why would it matter what people say about me? We feel
responsible. We want to be accepted by others. We live for
them, perpetually changing ourselves, but in fact if we feel
good with ourselves, everything works.

The broom
hanging
elsewhere.

I had spent some years with the same woman, and suddenly she went out to the street and in a direct encounter with crazy hormones, she telephoned me. "I've found the man of my life. I'm leaving. I can't stand you anymore!" A change in the program . . . she won't cook for me anymore, she won't wash my shirts, she won't take care of everything anymore while I go to my dreams; it's over. So you change companions. Another one comes.

She does the same as the one who left. You are happy. She washes your shirts, she mops the floor, but she won't leave the broom in the same place. She's going to look for her own place to leave the broom.

Everybody is different. No two people leave the broom in the same place. Nothing gets repeated. Nothing will ever be placed where it was, but we adapt to this new thing, and it is a great feeling. What a joy it is to adapt!

If life changes, we shouldn't fall apart over it. Everything that happens is for your own good. If there is a gap in your life, you think you won't ever fill it again, which in a way is true. You will never ever fill in something the same way, but other wonderful things will come if you adapt.

GLOSSARY

bonzo: Zen novice

dojo: meditation hall

hara: soft belly or abdomen, between the sternum and the pubis, including both vital organs and their functional energy fields

ikebana: the art of flower arrangement

keisaku: cane/warning stick/awakening stick used to refocus a meditator's attention

koan: a paradoxical riddle used to illustrate the futility of logical reasoning and provoke enlightenment

koromo: traditional outer monastic robe

mantra: a sound, word, or phrase that is repeated for meditation

mudra: a ritual spiritual gesture, often performed with the hands

shiragiku: white chrysanthemum

to: silence

zendo: a place for Zen meditation

INDEX

Takata, Ejo
  author's first meeting with, 2–3
  can given to author by, 4
  chair given to author by, 4
  characters on cane of, 5
  musical vibration of prayer by, 4
  on talking about good deeds, 5
  tarot reading for, 8
  Zen Rinzai school founding
    by, 1–2
Tangen, 95–98
Tanka, Master, 63–67
tarot, 8, 13, 42
Tchao-Tcheu Tests an Old
    Woman, 125
  Wu-Men's commentary, 126–38
Te-Chan, 119, 121–22
Ten Thousand, 105
Tenza, 51, 52, 55–56, 57–59
Test of the Jar, The, 27–28
The broom . . . , 157–58
The kitten . . . , 156
thirst, not quenched by concepts,
    36–37
Thomas, Saint, 108
Thousand Hands of the Buddha
    of Compassion, The,
    100–102
Three Worlds, The, 113
titles, 22
To cut her, what a pity! . . . , 154
Tokusan, 114–18

truth
  accepting not knowing, 56–57
  finding your own, 71
  levels of, 134
  seeking, 146
Two Cat Doors, The, 9–10
Two Monks and a Nightingale,
    51–59

Ummon, Master, 105, 106
U-Tsu, Master, 36–37

violet, living like a, 154
Visit of Master Tanka, The,
    63–67

warrior or samurai
  heaven and hell lesson for, 23
  his dog killed by, 29
  jar test for, 27–28
  old man and, 25–26
  paying attention by, 20
Water, 36–37
What Has Become of the Old
    Masters?, 114–18
What Is Buddha?, 38–40
Where Are You?, 82–83
white chrysanthemum, 148–49
White Stone, The, 60
women
  Buddhist distrust of, 128, 131
  spiteful, 136

BOOKS OF RELATED INTEREST

Sacred Trickery and the Way of Kindness
The Radical Wisdom of Jodo
by Alejandro Jodorowsky with Gilles Farcet

The Spiritual Journey of Alejandro Jodorowsky
The Creator of *El Topo*
by Alejandro Jodorowsky

The Way of Tarot
The Spiritual Teacher in the Cards
by Alejandro Jodorowsky and Marianne Costa

Psychomagic
The Transformative Power of Shamanic Psychotherapy
by Alejandro Jodorowsky

Manual of Psychomagic
The Practice of Shamanic Psychotherapy
by Alejandro Jodorowsky

The Dance of Reality
A Psychomagical Autobiography
by Alejandro Jodorowsky

Metagenealogy
Self-Discovery through Psychomagic and the Family Tree
by Alejandro Jodorowsky and Marianne Costa

Hara
The Vital Center of Man
by Karlfried Graf Dürckheim

INNER TRADITIONS • BEAR & COMPANY
P.O. Box 388 • Rochester, VT 05767
1-800-246-8648 • www.InnerTraditions.com

Or contact your local bookseller